EFFECTIVE PROTECTION OF HOUSEHOLD MEMBERS FROM VIOLENCE (ON THE BASIS OF POLISH LAW)

IRENEUSZ WOLWIAK

Title: ***EFFECTIVE PROTECTION OF HOUSEHOLD MEMBERS FROM VIOLENCE (ON THE BASIS OF POLISH LAW)***

ISBN: 979-8-89248-756-6

Author: IRENEUSZ WOLWIAK

Cover image: https://pixabay.com/

Publisher: Generis Publishing
Online orders: www.generis-publishing.com
Contact email: info@generis-publishing.com

Effective protection of household members from violence

(on the basis of Polish law)

Chapter I

Introductory remarks

Domestic violence is a violation of fundamental human rights, such as the right to life and health and respect for personal dignity. State authorities should therefore decide to introduce complex legal regulations that form the basis for counteracting the phenomena of that violence.

On 13 April 2015, the President of the Republic of Poland announced that the Council of Europe Convention on preventing and combating violence against women and domestic violence, whose wording he was making public, was opened for signature in Istanbul on 11 May 2011. Having become familiar with the content of the Convention, in the name of the Republic of Poland, the President also announced that: it has been recognized as valid both in its entirety and in each of its provisions; it has been accepted, ratified and confirmed; it will be maintained unchanged, taking into account the reservations set out in the declaration.

As proof of that, a legal instrument stamped with the presidential seal was issued by the President.[1] The Istanbul Convention became part of the Polish legal order as of 1 August 2015 in conjunction with the content of Article 91 item 1 of the Constitution of the Republic of Poland.[2]

At the time, the legal regulations of the Act of 29 July 2005 on counteracting family violence[3] were already in force in Poland to protect household members from violence, but they were insufficient in the light of the provisions of the Istanbul Convention.

---

[1] Journal of Laws 2015, item 961.

[2] Journal of Laws 197, No. 78, item 483.

Under Article 91 item 1 of the Constitution of the Republic of Poland, a ratified international agreement shall constitute part of the domestic legal order and shall be applied directly, unless its application depends on the enactment of a statute. Under Article 91 item 2, an international agreement ratified upon prior consent granted by statute shall have precedence over a statute if that statute cannot be reconciled with the agreement.

[3] Journal of Laws 2005, No. 180, item 1493; amended substantially by the Act of 10 June 2010 on amending the Act on counteracting family violence and certain other acts (Journal of Laws 2010, No. 125, item 842).

Article 29 of the Istanbul Convention prescribes that victims of any form of violence falling within its scope can make use of an adequate civil remedy against the perpetrator within the national legal system.[4]
Set to implement the provisions of the Convention, the Polish legislator chose to use the provisions already in force contained in various legal instruments and, at the same time, placed new regulations in them, considering that the existing legal protection based primarily on assistance from administrative authorities did not satisfy the requirements of the Convention. The provisions whose scope covers comprehensive legal regulation are laid down in the Act of 30 April 2020 on amending the Act – The Code of Civil Procedure and certain other acts.[5] Thus, the legislator imposed the obligation of taking actions to increase the effectiveness of steps counteracting incidents bearing the hallmarks of domestic violence first of all on administrative authorities.
The re-regulation of the situation providing protection from domestic violence was based on swift and efficient legal proceedings, which were separated in the Code of Civil Procedure. In parallel with court proceedings, the groundwork was laid for adequate police actions. For the immediate separation of a perpetrator of violence from other household members, the police were entitled to issue an administrative act ordering the perpetrator to vacate the dwelling or prohibiting him/her from approaching it. The validity of the order was limited to 14 days, but provision was made for its extension by the court. Even those regulations were insufficient to ensure the full protection of household members. Consequently, the legislator once again chose to modify primarily the provisions of the Code of Civil Procedure and the Police Act. Attention was paid to the situation of the perpetrator, who is obliged to vacate the dwelling immediately without the possibility of taking personal items or items related to professional work.

The Act of 13 January 2023[6] on amending the Act – the Code of Civil Procedure and certain other acts extended the police competences to include the possibility of issuing a prohibition on approach, a non-harassment order, and a prohibition on entering and remaining in certain localities. The court competences were also extended to include the possibility of delivering a ruling prohibiting the perpetrator from approaching a household member, prohibiting harassment or entering defined localities. The

---

[4] S. Spurek, *Nasza Konwencja*, Brussels 2023, p. 197 argued that Article 29 item 1 of the Convention prescribes that the Parties will take the necessary legislative or other measures to provide victims with adequate civil remedies against the perpetrator.
[5] Journal of Laws 2020, item 956.
[6] Journal of Laws 2023, item 289.

amendment covered court examination proceedings along with the introduction of separate provisions at the stage of enforcing a court ruling.

It seems that this area of legal regulation will provide significant protection from conduct involving domestic violence. In the case of conduct bearing the hallmarks of violence, being at the same time a prohibited act, the protection of household members is guaranteed within the framework of criminal proceedings. Under Article 12 item 2 of the Act of 13 January 2023, the legislator has imposed on all individuals who witness domestic violence the obligation to report it to police, a prosecutor or any other authority acting to counteract domestic violence.

Within the presented area of legal regulations involving the protection of household members from violence, it will be justified to single out for research analysis, first of all, State administrative actions in the form of authorizing the police to take immediate steps to isolate the perpetrator of violence.

Given an administrative act issued after a shortened procedure for determining the grounds for its issuance, the legal force of which expires after 14 days, it was necessary to prolong the situation involving the isolation of the perpetrator from household members. The protection is to be provided by a court order issued in court protection proceedings changed for the purposes of counteracting violence. Finally, the introduction of an order obliging the perpetrator of violence to vacate the dwelling or prohibiting him/her from approaching it, along with the possibility of issuing a prohibition on approaching, a non-harassment order, and a prohibition on entry, was left to the court's decision, which, after conducting examination proceedings, would issue a ruling indicating appropriate conduct to the perpetrator of violence. This order will finally make it possible to carry out another procedure governed by the Code of Civil Procedure. It is judicial enforcement proceedings, in which a court enforcement officer, using coercive measures, can enforce a court ruling. In this way, the scope of legal regulations intended to ensure the protection of household members affected by violence creates an effective area of counteracting such phenomena.

The presented issues are connected with court proceedings and will be the subject of analysis in the individual chapters to examine the functionality of the introduced measures and draw conclusions as to the correctness of the existing regulation. This will also allow for an assessment of the implementation of the provisions of the Istanbul Convention, bearing in mind that Article 52 of the Convention prescribes that the Parties shall take the necessary legislative or other measures to ensure that the competent authorities are granted the power to order, in situations of immediate danger, a perpetrator of domestic violence to vacate the residence of the victim or person at risk for a sufficient period of time and to prohibit the perpetrator from entering the residence of or contacting the victim or person at risk. Measures taken by the Parties pursuant to this article shall give priority to the safety of victims or persons at risk.

In turn, Article 53 item 1 of the Istanbul Convention imposes on the Parties the obligation in the form of taking the necessary legislative or other measures to ensure that appropriate restraining or protection orders are available to victims of all forms of violence covered by the scope of the Convention. Such restraining or protection orders are available for immediate protection without undue financial or administrative burdens placed on the victim, even though they will be issued for a specified period or until modified or discharged. Additional protection is given by the possibility of issuing them on an ex parte basis with an immediate effect, irrespective of other, running in parallel or possible to be initiated, legal proceedings. The Parties shall take the necessary legislative or other measures to ensure that breaches of restraining or protection orders shall be subject to effective, proportionate and dissuasive criminal or other legal sanctions.

Such an order or prohibition of specified conduct is intended to be a complementary measure to a short-term police-issued summary order. It is designed as a swift legal remedy for individuals at risk of any form of violence defined in the Convention.[7] It is required that an order or prohibition lay down immediate protection, be available without undue financial and administrative burdens. They are to be immediately enforceable upon issuance and available without lengthy legal proceedings.[8]

A restraining or protection order can be issued only at the request of one of the parties. The issuing of a restraining or protection order must not violate the rights of the defence and the requirements for a fair and impartial trial.[9]

The submission of an application for a restraining or protection order must not be made dependent on initiating criminal proceedings or other proceedings, such as divorce proceedings. Conversely, the conduct of criminal or other civil proceedings in the same matter against the same perpetrator shall not be an obstacle to issuing a restraining or protection order.[10]

Article 3 point b of the Istanbul Convention defines domestic violence as all acts of physical, sexual, psychological or economic violence that occur within the family or

---

[7] S. Spurek, *Nasza Konwencja...*, p. 239.

[8] S. Spurek, *Nasza Konwencja...*, p. 239.

[9] S. Spurek, *Nasza Konwencja...*, p. 240.

[10] S. Spurek, *Nasza Konwencja...*, p. 241.

domestic unit or between former or current spouses or partners, whether or not the perpetrator shares or has shared the same residence with the victim. When interpreting this provision, it should be noted that domestic violence mentioned in the Convention essentially comprises two types of violence: violence occurring between former or current spouses or partners and intergenerational violence typically occurring between parents and children. Violence continues after the (marital or parental) relationship ends, so the cohabitation of victim and perpetrator is not required. This instrument envisages a broader legal protection for women, who in practice are the most frequent victims of domestic violence.[11]

A legal definition of domestic violence is also laid down in Article 2 item 1 point 1 letters a-e of the Act on counteracting domestic violence, which provides that domestic violence should be understood as a single or repeated intentional action or omission that takes physical, mental or economic advantage and violates the rights or personal goods of a person experiencing domestic violence. It particularly includes actions or omissions exposing that person to the danger of a loss of life, health or property; violating that person's dignity, bodily integrity or freedom, including sexual freedom; causing physical or mental damage, suffering or harm in that person; restricting or depriving that person of financial means or opportunities for gaining employment or financial independence; significantly invading that person's privacy or causing that person to feel threatened, humiliated or anguished, including those undertaken by means of electronic communication.

It is the first definition of the term in the provisions of Polish universally binding law. When developing that provision, the drafters were inspired by a working definition specifying that domestic violence is an intentional action taking advantage of superiority of force directed against a family member, which violates personal rights and goods, causing damage and suffering. This means that in the case of family violence, the most significant elements are the demonstration and use of force or power in a way that is harmful to other family members. It is marked with intentionalism and the perpetrator's existing intent. Violence may be a single or repeated conduct undertaken as a result of action or omission.[12]

The examination of the effective protection of household members from violence carried out in the following part of the study will be limited to police actions within the scope of competences laid down in the Police Act and the Act on Administrative Enforcement Proceedings and the steps taken by the court and the court enforcement authority based on the provisions of civil procedural law. The research activities will

[11] E. Bieńkowska, L. Mazowiecka, *Konwencja o zapobieganiu i zwalczaniu przemocy domowej wobec kobiet,* Warsaw 2016, Lex/el, marginal note 6 to Article 3 point b of the Convention.

[12] S. Spurek, *Przeciwdziałanie przemocy w rodzinie Komentarz,* Warsaw 2019, pp. 93-95.

be performed using the dogmatic method based on the provisions of law in force in Poland, including the provisions of the Istanbul Convention, taking into account **the** decision of the Council of the European Union and the legislative resolution of the European Parliament on the accession of the European Union to that Convention. The performed research activities will also apply the rules of formal logic with elements of legal criticism and an analysis of data included in a report of the Council of Ministers on the Implementation of the Government Programme of Counteracting Domestic Violence.

Chapter II

Police protection from domestic violence

2.1. The issuing of an administrative act

The police are a public authority that most frequently encounters situations of domestic violence. Regardless of whether a notification of the need to intervene came from household members or from third parties, a police intervention arises primarily from the obligation to protect human life and health from unlawful attacks violating these goods (Article 1 item 2 point 1 of the Police Act).[13] Thus the application of measures counteracting domestic violence involves a police intervention directly at the scene of an incident. Moreover, it will be possible to issue an administrative act in a police authority regarding protection from domestic violence as a result of the previously performed actions establishing the fact of the use of violence (Article 15ab item 1 PA).

The science of administrative law introduced the expression: administrative police. It allows for the indication of a specific relationship between the individual and public administrative authorities acting to protect goods such as public safety, public order, public peace – or values in the form of life and health.[14]

Establishing the facts at the scene of intervention, which point to the use of violence, will enable police officers to qualify such a factual situation as domestic violence and take steps to eliminate the danger posed to the household members. The Police Act provides for the possibility that the police issue an adequate legal instrument in respect of the perpetrator of domestic violence who poses a threat to the life or health of the person experiencing violence.

In such a situation the police are also entitled to detain a person, but it can take place only when that person clearly poses an imminent threat to human life or health and to property (Article 15 item 1 point 3 PA). In addition to the permissibility of detaining

[13] Act of 6 April 1990; (Consolidated) Journal of Laws 2024, item 145, hereinafter PA.

[14] M. Janik [in:] *Administracja Prawo administracyjne Część ogólna*, eds. J. Blicharz, L. Zacharko, Katowice 2018, p. 307.

such a person under Article 15a PA, this entitlement can be exercised when a perpetrator of violence poses an imminent threat to human life or health.[15]

The grounds for a police officer to issue an administrative act is a situation where a perpetrator of domestic violence, within the meaning of the provisions of the Act on Counteracting Domestic Violence, poses a threat to the life or health of a person experiencing violence (Article 15aa item 1 PA)

It is also up to a police officer to make an assessment of the grounds for detention. The decision depends on the identification of an imminent threat to the life or health of an immediate family member or any other person living together or maintaining a common household with the perpetrator of violence. The threat must therefore be real, objective and imminent.[16] There is no doubt about the police's authority to detain perpetrators of violence that pose an imminent threat to life and death.[17] When a perpetrator of domestic violence is detained, an administrative act on the protection of household members is issued immediately after his/her release (Article 15ab item 2 sentence 1 PA). A police officer may issue an order to vacate immediately the jointly occupied dwelling and its immediate surroundings and a prohibition on approaching the jointly occupied dwelling and its immediate surroundings (Article 15aa item 1 PA). The Police Act grants the authority to issue that administrative act to every police officer.

The issuing of an order to vacate the dwelling jointly occupied with a person affected by violence and the prohibition on approaching the dwelling aims to provide safety for the person experiencing domestic violence both in terms of direct and visual contact.[18]

An order and a prohibition issued by a police officer is an administrative act.[19] It contains a specified expression of conduct prescribed for an individually designated

---

[15] It has been argued that Article 15a PA did not introduce any significant new quality to the protection of victims of domestic violence. Detention by police is provided for in Article 244 § 1a and 1 b of the Code of Criminal Procedure. Therefore, the provision of Article 15a PA is a manifestation of some type of over-regulation and coexistence of provisions that are not properly linked to each other – J. Karaźniewicz [in:] *Ustawa o Policji. Komentarz*, eds. K. Chałubińska-Jentkiewicz, J. Kurek, Warsaw 2021, marginal note 1 to Article 15a.

[16] J. Karaźniewicz [in:] *Ustawa o Policji...*, marginal note 3 to Article 15a.

[17] W. Kotowski, *Ustawa o Policji. Komentarz* , Lex/el 2024, comment 1 to Article 15a.

[18] P. Łabuz [in:] *Ustawa o Policji Komentarz*, ed. A. Choromańska, Warsaw 2022, marginal note 1 to Article 15aa.

[19] The administrative act is most frequently referred to as a unilateral, authoritative, external declaration of will or knowledge of a public administrative authority, which is addressed to a non-

person when faced with the occurrence of facts that fulfil the hypothesis of a substantive law standard.[20] The hypothesis of that standard is formed by facts creating situations that are incidents of domestic violence as defined in Article 2 item 1 point 1 of the Act of 29 July 2005 on Counteracting Domestic Violence,[21] taking into account the persons in respect of whom such acts may take place (mentioned in Article 2 item 1 point 2 and item 2 ACDV), with the simultaneous qualification of such facts as posing a threat to the life or health of a person experiencing violence.

Such a decision can be made after an adequate procedure has been carried out, during which circumstances proving the conduct bearing the hallmarks of domestic violence should be shown, together with the determination of the existence of a threat to the life or health of persons affected by violence. Under the procedure, witnesses will be questioned in accordance with the provisions of the Code of Civil Procedure[22] (Articles 259-277 Code of Civil Procedure). Other steps leading to the establishment of the grounds for issuing an order may also be taken. The police may require additional information from institutions or authorities (Article 15 ab items 4-9 and 11 PA). The person reporting domestic violence shall also be questioned. The reporting person shall be questioned as a witness as to the circumstances indicated in the notification (Article 15ab item 4 PA). To make the assessment, a police officer shall use a relevant form,[23] which is to facilitate the conduct of procedure.

A decision to issue an order and a prohibition is made after carrying out the actions specified in Article 15 ab PA. Administrative acts are issued in a procedure consisting of a sequence of procedural acts undertaken for a specific purpose. The administrative procedure aims to ensure its uniform and predictable course in the process of applying substantive law, the implementation and giving effect to substantive law and to ensure

---

subordinate, individualized actor and is aimed at resolving a specific administrative matter – E. Pierzchała [in:] *Administracja Prawo administracyjne Część ogólna*, eds. J. Blicharz, L. Zacharko, Katowice 2018, p. 193 (whose parts the author discusses further on pp. 193 – 195).

[20] For more, see I. Wolwiak, *Zabezpieczenie rodziny przed przemocą w następstwie wydanego przez Policję nakazu opuszczenia mieszkania bądź zbliżania się do niego*, Acta Univeristatis Lodziensis Folia Iuridica 2023, special number, pp. 359 – 370.

[21] (Consolidated) Journal of Laws 2024, item 424: hereinafter ACDV.

[22] Act of 17 November 1964, (Consolidated) Journal of Laws 2024, item 1568; hereinafter CCP.

[23] G. Wrona, *Ustawa o przeciwdziałaniu przemocy w rodzinie. Komentarz*, Legalis/el 2021, marginal note 26 to Article 11a; P. Piskozub, *Izolacja sprawcy przemocy w rodzinie*, Legalis/el 2021, comment 3 in Chapter 3.

and respect the rights and freedoms protected by the Constitution of the Republic of Poland.[24]

The scope of a substantive decision of the police was extended by the introduction of permissibility of issuing further prohibitions in respect of a perpetrator of domestic violence (Article 15aaa items 1 and 2 PA[25]) in the form of a prohibition on approaching the person experiencing violence closer than a distance prescribed in metres (designated as prohibition on approach) or a prohibition on contacting the person experiencing violence (designated as prohibition on contact), and a prohibition on entering the premises of a school, educational, care, artistic, sports facility, a workplace or any other locality accompanied by a prohibition on the perpetrator's presence on those premises (designated as prohibition on entry). Specifically, the prohibition on entry applies to a situation where a person experiencing violence attends school, an educational, care or artistic facility, does sport or performs work, provided that the perpetrator of violence does not work or take classes there.

The basis for issuing a prohibition on approach, a prohibition on contact and a prohibition on entry in respect of a perpetrator of domestic violence is the conduct that poses a threat to the life or health of the person experiencing that violence (Article 15aaa items 1 and 2 PA).

In a situation where, after an order and a prohibition to vacate the dwelling has been issued, circumstances arise that justify taking such a decision, a police officer is empowered to issue a prohibition on approach, contact or entry in respect of the perpetrator of domestic violence. However, the end date of those prohibitions must correspond to the day on which the previously issued order to vacate the dwelling and the prohibition on approaching it expires (Article 15aab item 3 PA).

All the mentioned orders and prohibitions may be applied jointly (Article 15aab item 1 PA). It is also envisaged that the police may issue an order to vacate the dwelling and a prohibition on approaching it in the case where a prohibition on approach and contact has already been issued, even though it is not provided for in Article 15aab PA. Authors argue that an order to vacate the dwelling and a prohibition on approaching it will then be in force longer than the 14-day period of a prohibition on approach and contact.[26] One must share the argument on the possibility of issuing an order to vacate the

---

[24] E. Pierzchała [in:] *Administracja…*, p. 196.

[25] Which took place by means of the Act of 13 January 2023 – see footnote number 6.

[26] G. Wrona [in:] *Przeciwdziałanie przemocy domowej – analiza zmian*, P. Piskozub, G. Wrona, Warsaw 2023, pp. 108-109.

dwelling and a prohibition on approaching it at the time when the prohibitions on approach, contact or entry are in force, but when a legal standard is derived by *legis analogia* from the content of Article 15aab items 1 and 3 PA, the date of expiry of all orders and prohibitions may not be longer than 14 days. It is not admissible to re-issue an order to vacate the dwelling and a prohibition on approaching it or extend its duration without a court order delivered in protection proceedings (Article 755^2 § 1 CCP).

Ensuring the effective protection of household members from violence in this case involves the introduction of immediate enforceability of an order to vacate the dwelling and a prohibition on approaching it, a prohibition on approach, a prohibition on contact and a prohibition on entry issued by the police (Article 15aab item 2 PA). Notably, both the order to vacate the dwelling and the prohibition on approaching it and the prohibition on approach, the prohibition on contact and the prohibition on entry expire after 14 days (Article 15ak item 1 PA).

The decision-making by police is facilitated by the circumstances listed in Article 15a item 2 PA, which will support the issuing of an order to vacate the dwelling and a prohibition on approaching it and the other prohibitions in connection with a reference to the provision indicating the grounds for making a decision on detention (Article 15aaab item 4 PA).

2.2. The nature of conducted procedure

The Act does not designate the procedure carried out by police. It does not provide for any reference to the application of other provisions either. It only provides for a reference to the correct application of the strictly specified provisions of the Code of Civil Procedure and the Criminal Code. A person reporting family violence is questioned as a witness (Article 15aa item 4 sentence 1 PA), having been instructed under Article 233 of the Criminal Code[27] (about the commission of a prohibited act in the case of false testimony or concealing the truth). The taking of evidence from witness testimony is carried out in accordance with the provisions of the Code of Civil Procedure on the taking of such evidence (Article 15aa item 5 PA).

The legislator introduced a name for the decision taken by the police using the terms "order and prohibition". The decision taken by the police was given the following

---

[27] Act of 6 June1997, (Consolidated) Journal of Laws 2024, item 17: hereinafter CC.

wording: the order to vacate immediately the jointly occupied dwelling and its immediate surroundings and the prohibition on approaching the jointly occupied dwelling and its immediate surroundings (Article 15aa item 1 PA). The other police-issued prohibitions were also given a name. One can assume that it will be a legal instrument issued by a state authority, being a sovereign legal action of a public administrative authority, which designates an individually defined obligation of specified conduct imposed on the addressee of the act. It is a manifestation of the will of an individual or individuals representing the authority and it is directed to produce specified, individually defined effects.[28] This action is related to the specified objective, which is to protect the values of life and health and the public interest – it fits in with the operation of so-called administrative police.[29]

The characteristic features of an administrative act can be specified as follows: it is an act based on legal premises; it is a sovereign declaration of will of an administrative authority; it is issued as a result of an administrative procedure; with double specification; it may produce effects not only in the area of administrative law but also in other areas of law.[30]

Despite the lack of a name for the procedure, it is important to emphasize the close relationship between the procedure for issuing an administrative act and substantive law, or more precisely, the dependence of the shape of procedural institutes on the substantive regulation.[31] Substantive law standards can be achieved only as an organized action being a sequence of undertaken legal and factual steps, each of which has a specified place and consequence in that action.[32]

The interdependence between substantive law and procedural law stems from the fact that a standard derived from substantive law provisions contains a factual situation in its hypothesis, whereas procedural law rules determine conduct in terms of identification of the factual circumstances of the case, allowing for its subsumption within a constructed hypothesis. This makes it possible to issue a decision specifying

---

[28]E. Ochendowski, *Prawo administracyjne część ogólna*, Toruń 2013, p. 195.

[29]M. Janik [in:] *Administracja...*, pp. 397 -326.

[30]L. Bielecki [in:] *Prawo administracyjne Część ogólna, ustrojowe prawo administracyjne, wybrane zagadnienia materialnego prawa administracyjnego*, eds. M. Zdyb, J. Stelmasiak, Warsaw 2016, p. 203.

[31]B. Adamiak, *Zagadnienia ogólne procesowego prawa administracyjnego* [in:] *System prawa administracyjnego, Vol. 9. Prawo procesowe administracyjne*, eds. R. Hauser, Z. Niewiadomski, A. Wróbel Warsaw 2020, p.16; B. Adamiak, *Postępowanie administracyjne i sądowoadministracyjne*, Warsaw 2021, 27.

[32] B. Adamiak, *Zagadnienia ogólne...*, p. 3.

the command regarding the conduct of the addressee of a legal standard, provided that the factual situation is correctly identified.[33] The interdependence between substantive law and procedural law is particularly important for the implementation of the constitutional principle of a democratic state of law. One of the basic constitutional values is to ensure that the individual defends his/her legal interest through proceedings regulated by law.[34] The legislator introduced separate provisions governing the course of an examination of the basis for issuing an order and a prohibition (prohibitions). In the event of information about a situation of domestic violence, it is important to take immediate action. It is necessary to strike a balance between the scope of action to establish the facts concerning violence, giving necessary assistance to household members and the efficiency of the procedure.

It will be useful for the qualification of the procedure carried out by the police to adopt the concept of administrative procedure as relating solely to proceedings with a single subject-matter concerning the authoritative specification of a standard of substantive administrative law.[35] The specificity of an administrative act is expressed by reference both to its addressee and his/her conduct.[36] It is possible to formulate the following definition of administrative procedure: "an organised sequence of acts of competent public administrative authorities and other actors in the procedure undertaken with a view to examine and adjudicate on a case by specifying authoritatively a standard of substantive law."[37]

The police-issued order and prohibition is not an administrative decision issued as a consequence of carrying out a procedure under the provisions of the Code of Administrative Procedure[38] but an act of the application of substantive law. It is a sovereign act of a State authority, though it should be added that the Code of Administrative Procedure does not contain a full codification of administrative procedure. Its dissimilarities are placed in special laws, some of which are even considered to be a separate mode of administrative procedure.[39]

---

[33] See B. Adamiak, *Zagadnienia ogólne*...,16; Z. Kmiecik, *Wszczęcie ogólnego postępowania administracyjnego*, Warsaw 2014, p. 19.

[34] B. Adamiak, *Zagadnienia ogólne*..., p. 16.

[35] B. Adamiak, *Zagadnienia ogólne*..., p. 12.

[36] E. Szewczyk, M. Szewczyk, *Generalny akt administracyjny między indywidualnym aktem administracyjnym a aktem normatywnym*, Warsaw 2014, pp. 104-105.

[37] B. Adamiak, *Zagadnienia ogólne*..., 16).

[38] Act of 14 June 1960, (Consolidated) Journal of Laws 2024, item 572.

[39] A. Hauser, W. Piątek, A. Paduch, A Skoczylas [in:] *Postępowanie administracyjne i sądowoadministracyjne*, eds. A. Hauser, A. Skoczylas, Warsaw 2021, p. 28.

2.3. Guarantee of access to the court for the perpetrator of violence

The order to vacate immediately the jointly occupied dwelling and its immediate surroundings and the prohibition on approaching the jointly occupied dwelling and its immediate surroundings (Article 15aa item 1 PA) provide a guideline on the conduct of a perpetrator of violence, who is deprived of the possibility of using the dwelling. The order is independent of any legal title the perpetrator may have to the dwelling. Meanwhile, public authorities are to pursue policies conducive to satisfying the housing needs of citizens, in particular combating homelessness (Article 75 item 1 of the Constitution of the Republic of Poland). The Polish Constitution protects the rights of tenants (Article 75 item 2 of the Constitution of the Republic of Poland). The law makes it necessary to obtain a court ruling for the possibility of ordering someone to vacate and clear the dwelling (Articles 14 -17 of the Act of 21 June 2001 on the protection of tenants' rights, the housing stock of a commune and an amendment to the Civil Code).[40]

However, Article 31 item 3 sentence 1 of the Constitution of the Republic of Poland prescribes that any restriction upon the exercise of constitutional freedoms and rights may be imposed only by statute, and only when necessary in a democratic state for the protection of its security or public order, or to protect the natural environment, health and public morals, or the freedom and rights of others. At the same time, Article 52 sentence 2 of the Istanbul Convention lays down that measures taken pursuant to Article 52 sentence 1 of the Convention shall give priority to the safety of victims or persons at risk.

In turn, Article 77 item 2 of the Constitution of the Republic of Poland prescribes that statutes shall not bar anyone's right of access to the court in pursuit of claims alleging an infringement of freedoms and rights. Ordinary courts shall implement the administration of justice in all matters, save for those statutorily reserved for other courts (Article 177 of the Constitution of the Republic of Poland). For the introduction of such safeguards in the case of a person in respect of whom an order and a prohibition, a prohibition on approach, a prohibition on contact or a prohibition on entry has been issued, the admissibility of lodging a complaint by that person against a police-issued decision is envisaged. The complaint is brought before the district court competent to hear domestic violence cases. The complaint is lodged within 3 days from the date of service of an order and a prohibition, a prohibition on approach, a prohibition on contact or a prohibition on entry, of which the perpetrator of domestic violence must

[40] (Consolidated) Journal of Laws 2023, item 725.

be instructed at the time of service (Article 15aj item 1 sentence 1 and 2 PA). The Police Act regulates in detail the action of serving a copy of such a legal instrument on a person in respect of whom an order and a prohibition, a prohibition on approach, a prohibition on contact or a prohibition on entry has been issued. The public prosecutor is also entitled to lodge a complaint. A copy of an order and a prohibition, a prohibition on approach, a prohibition on contact or a prohibition on entry is served *ex officio* on the public prosecutor by the police.

In this way, the law opens the way to pursue claims alleging an infringement of freedoms and rights in the court for a person in respect of whom an order and a prohibition, a prohibition on approach, a prohibition on contact or a prohibition on entry has been issued (Article 77 item 2 of the Constitution of the Republic of Poland). The person may require that the court examine the correctness of performed actions and the validity and legality of an issued order and prohibition, prohibition on approach, prohibition on contact or prohibition on entry. The appeal is heard pursuant to the provisions of the Code of Civil Procedure in non-contentious proceedings.

The interested actor must be given the possibility of initiating proceedings before the court to assess the validity of a decision taken by a non-court authority.[41] It is not always necessary that a court hears a case and delivers a ruling within the meaning of the right of access to the court defined in Article 45 item 1 of the Polish Constitution.[42] The proceedings may be carried out by authorities other than courts established to resolve disputes over rights. The Constitution of the Republic of Poland does not exclude such action, but then it is required that proceedings can be initiated before the court to examine the validity of the decision.

The Constitutional Tribunal formulated a view that the right of access to the court – by the initiation of proceedings before a common or administrative court – is respected under such regulations that provide for a judicial review of a ruling, decision, or other

---

[41] P. Grzegorczyk, K. Weitz [in:] *Konstytucja RP. T. 1. Komentarz. Art. 1–86.* eds. M. Safjan, L. Bosek, Warsaw 2016, p. 1118.

[42] The consideration of a case as a concept of the expression laid down in this provision involves a decision on the rights or obligations of an actor on the basis of legal norms derived from legal provisions. The essence of the consideration of a case is the legal qualification of a specified factual situation, contained in an issued specific and individual norm, addressed to a specific actor, from which certain rights or obligations arise. (see a judgement of the Constitutional Tribunal of 13 March 2012, P 39/10, OTK-A 2012, No. 3, item 26).

individual act shaping the legal situation of an actor.[43] However, courts must always hold a superior position allowing for a review of a decision taken by a non-court authority.[44]

Within the unregulated scope, the provisions of the Code of Civil Procedure on non-contentious proceedings apply accordingly to the complaint. The proceedings are to take place swiftly, therefore actions involving other individuals have been excluded, including those who have endured violence. They are not even served a copy of the complaint. The law provides only for the participation of the authority that issued an order and a prohibition, a prohibition on approach, a prohibition on contact or a prohibition on entry. The public prosecutor participates only if he or she lodged the complaint. The law provides for the participation of the public prosecutor in complaint proceedings (as an entity of those proceedings pursuant to Article 510 § 1 and 2 CCP), but it is no impediment for the public prosecutor to join the complaint proceedings pursuant to Article 60 § 1 CCP. This general entitlement to join any case was based on the prosecutor's presence in it without any connection to any parties or participants in the proceedings.

A complaint is efficiently examined thanks to the panel consisting of one judge and the content of the provision on immediate examination, that is, no later than within 3 days from the date of its receipt by the court.

2.4. Examination of the complaint

The court examines the correctness of performed actions and the validity and legality of an issued order and prohibition, prohibition on approach, prohibition on contact or prohibition on entry. The first basis of the examination relates to the actions taken by a police officer in terms of the provisions of the Police Act. Where the entirety of this specific administrative procedure is exhausted by the actions provided for in the Police Act, the remaining step is to analyse the undertaken actions in accordance with the rules for their implementation. It is primarily the action of determining the factual situation in the area of facts arising from the hypothesis of a legal norm. It is therefore necessary to examine the procedure as to the taking of evidence from witness

[43] Judgement of the Constitutional Tribunal of 2 June 1999, K 34/98, OTK 1999, No. 5, item 94; Judgement of the Constitutional Tribunal of 4 March 2008, SK 3/07, OTK-A 2008, No. 2, item 25; Judgement of the Constitutional Tribunal of 13 March 2012, P 39/10, OTK-A 2012, No. 3, item 26.
[44] Judgement of the Constitutional Tribunal of 4 March 2008, SK 3/07 OTK-A 2008, No. 2, item 25.

testimony, having regard to the provisions of the Code of Civil Procedure on the taking of such evidence (Article 15ab items 4 and 5 PA). The hearing of a perpetrator of violence is not regulated (Article 15ab item 9 PA), though given the ancillary importance of that action, it will be a simple opportunity to obtain a statement without the introduction of formal conditions for its implementation, such as giving instruction about the consequences of that action.

Regardless of the conduct of the examination, even in the case of a possible infringement of any provision of the Code of Civil Procedure or the Code of Criminal Procedure, the court will have to decide whether, and if so how, that infringement could affect the police-issued decision imposing an order and a prohibition on vacating the dwelling, a prohibition on approach, a prohibition on contact or a prohibition on entry. Apart from a reference to the application of the provisions of the Code of Civil Procedure to the complaint, the Police Act makes no further provisions. It would be justified now to produce a scientific proof as regards the possibility and scope of appropriate application of the provisions of another legal instrument to the situation under analysis. Given the breadth of the issue, it is appropriate to make a reference to the views expressed in the literature[45] and present the basic theses resulting from its postulates. Three groups of situations can be distinguished for the proper application of the provisions of law. The first group comprises situations where the proper application consists of the use of relevant provisions without any modifications. The second group comprises situations where the relevant provisions may be used with certain modifications. The third group comprises provisions which, due to their pointlessness or inconsistency with the provisions established for the relationships to which they were to be applied accordingly, cannot be applied at all.[46]

The validity and legality of the issued order and prohibition, prohibition on approach, prohibition on contact or prohibition on entry are the next grounds for a police-issued decision subjected to a court assessment as part of complaint proceedings. The legality of an issued order and prohibition means that an administrative act was issued based on the Police Act by a police officer. Under Article 15aa item 1 PA, a police officer shall determine the conduct of the perpetrator of domestic violence by putting an abstract-general standard authoritatively into effect. The decision taken will result in the creation of a legal relationship with direct effects falling within the scope of law.[47]

---

[45] J. Nowacki, *„Odpowiednie" stosowanie; Analogia legis*, Warsaw 1966, pp. 367-376; I. Wolwiak, *Odpowiednie stosowanie przepisów o procesie do samodzielnego postępowania uregulowanego w KPC*, Monitor Prawniczy 2021, No. 8, pp. 413-414.

[46] Order of the Supreme Court of 8 November 2023, II UZ 47/23, Legalis/el, No. 3005851.

[47] M. Zdyb, *Istota decyzji*, Lublin 1993, p. 140.

At the same time, its assessment in terms of rationality and efficiency will also be possible.[48]

An administrative act will be issued when a police officer establishes facts that fulfil the hypothesis of a legal standard whose disposition includes an order to vacate the dwelling and a prohibition on approaching it, a prohibition on approaching the person experiencing violence or contacting him/her, or entering defined localities. A police-issued decision will not be qualified as legal without a factual basis for its issuance. Similarly, a decision issued in the event of incidents bearing the hallmarks of violence, as defined in Article 2 item 1 point 1 and item 2 ACDV, will be considered illegal (contrary to law) without showing that there was a threat to the life or health of individuals affected by violence (Article 15aa item 1 PA). It is pointed out that the threat to life or health must be real and objective. It cannot be based solely on the subjective feelings and declarations of a person for whose protection an order or prohibitions are intended. Such threat is analysed based on the circumstance relating to situations of violence. These include acts involving violence, the specific characteristics of individuals against whom violence was used and a perpetrator of violence, and the circumstances relating to the conduct bearing the hallmarks of violence.[49]

In turn, the validity of a police-issued decision relates to a properly applied legal measure aimed at protecting a person from violence in connection with the factual findings made in the case. First of all, validity will relate to the most severe measure taken by the police, that is, an order to vacate the dwelling and a prohibition on approaching it. The above remarks on the encroachment by a police-issued act on the entitlement of a perpetrator of violence to occupy the dwelling, which forces the perpetrator to seek new accommodation for at least 14 days, requires a careful analysis of the circumstances of the incident. It is an additional burden on an employee who has to fulfil his/her work obligations in a situation of being suddenly deprived of dwelling. Although the police are to provide information on the contact details of locally appropriate accommodation providers and providers of correctional-educational and psychological-therapeutic programmes for perpetrators of violence (Article 15ah PA), an assessment of the validity of an adopted measure will make it possible to impose, instead of an order to vacate the dwelling and a prohibition on approaching it, a prohibition on approaching the person affected by violence closer than a distance prescribed in metres or a prohibition on contact with the person experiencing violence

[48] For more, see M. Zdyb, *Istota...*, pp. 186-215.

[49] J. Karaźniewicz [in:] *Ustawa o Policji…*, marginal number 3 to Article 15aa.

(Article 15aaa item 1 PA) or a prohibition on entering the premises of a school, educational, care, artistic, sports facility or a workplace accompanied by a prohibition on the perpetrator's presence on those premises (Article 15aaa item 2 PA).

In the absence of any indication in the Police Act of other rulings issued by the court after the examination of a complaint, it must be concluded that the court will be empowered to dismiss an appeal brought by a perpetrator of violence or a public prosecutor if it is unfounded (Article 385 in conjunction with Article 397 § 3 CCP and Article 394^{1a} § 2 CCP in conjunction with Article 13 § 2 CCP). In that case, the legislator relies on the institute of reference to the provisions of law. In the unregulated scope, the provisions of the Code of Civil Procedure on non-contentious proceedings apply accordingly to the complaint.

This method of regulating a specific issue by cross-reference provisions in the strict sense is a technical measure for shortening the legal text when, instead of repeating the text of a provision, the references refer to it by an indication of the number of an article, paragraph or other designation of a legal text containing a provision.[50] At the same time, in view of the features differentiating the situation regulated in the provisions of a referral, it is a proper application of provisions.[51]

The court will also be empowered to issue an order repealing a contested administrative act (Article 386 § 4 in conjunction with Article 397 § 3 CCP and Article 394^{1a} § 2 CCP in conjunction with Article 397 § 2 and Article 13 § 2 CCP). Moreover, the court will be empowered to change the content of the ruling laid down in an order and a prohibition and in the prohibitions (Article 386 § 1 CCP in conjunction with Article 397 § 3 CCP and Article 394^{1a} § 2 in conjunction with Article 13 § 2 CCP).

In the absence of any other regulation in the Police Act, attention should be paid to the possibility that the court may suspend the enforceability of an issued order and prohibition, prohibition on approach, prohibition on contact or prohibition on entry in the case where a complaint is lodged together with an application for the suspension of enforceability of the order and prohibition (Article 396 CCP in conjunction with Article 394^{1a} § 2 CCP).

It is emphasized that the proper application of the regulation on issuing an order and a prohibition (prohibitions) requires knowledge and skills among police officers,

---

[50] J. Wróblewski [in:] *Jerzy Wróblewski pisma wybrane*, wybór i wstęp M. Zirk-Sadowski, Warsaw 2015, p. 267.

[51] See the above remarks on the proper application of provisions.

allowing for an appropriate level of initiative, decision-making but also assertiveness to counter situations of abuse of those provisions.[52] Authors point out that the issuing of an order and a prohibition is in a sense a breach of the principle of the presumption of innocence arising from Article 5 § 1 of the Code of Penal Procedure.[53] It seriously breaches the personal rights of the person in respect of whom it is issued, but it is not unlawful. It is therefore necessary to apply those provisions with a great deal of insight and competence.[54]

Between 1 January 2022 and 31 December 2022, the police officers of the particular units of the police issued 4,960 orders to vacate immediately the jointly occupied dwelling and its immediate surroundings and prohibitions on approaching the jointly occupied dwelling and its immediate surroundings, broken down into:

– 120 orders to vacate immediately the jointly occupied dwelling and its immediate surroundings;

– 263 prohibitions on approaching the jointly occupied dwelling and its immediate surroundings;

– 4,577 orders to vacate immediately the jointly occupied dwelling and its immediate surroundings and prohibitions on approaching the jointly occupied dwelling and its immediate surroundings.[55]

---

[52] M. Burtowy, *Nowa procedura szybkiego reagowania wobec sprawców przemocy domowej*, Lex/el 2020, point 2.1

[53] Act of 6 June 1997, (Consolidated) Journal of Laws 2024, item 37: hereinafter CPP.

[54] M. Burtowy, *Nowa procedura…*, point 2.1.

[55] A report of the Council of Ministers on the Implementation of the Government Programme of Counteracting Domestic Violence for the Sejm and Senate of the Republic of Poland.

Chapter III

Enforcement of police-issued orders and prohibitions

A police-issued order to vacate immediately the jointly occupied dwelling and its immediate surroundings and a prohibition on approaching the jointly occupied dwelling and its immediate surroundings are not equivalent to the physical isolation of a perpetrator of violence from the individuals staying on the premises. It is necessary to examine the admissibility of forcing a perpetrator of violence to vacate the dwelling or to prohibit the perpetrator from approaching it. No provisions involving such actions were included in the Police Act or the Act on Counteracting Domestic Violence. The need arises to assess the scope of police's competence to perform actions in the sphere of protecting family members from incidents of violence, given that the police have been empowered to issue an order to vacate immediately the jointly occupied dwelling and its immediate surroundings and a prohibition on approaching the jointly occupied dwelling and its immediate surroundings. Imposing on the perpetrator of violence an obligation to behave in a specified manner, which may be carried out using coercive measures, involves moving the discussion on to administrative enforcement proceedings. The actions taken to enforce a specific conduct in connection with decisions made by administrative authorities are defined in the Act of 17 June 1966 on Administrative Enforcement Proceedings.[56]

Ensuring that State authorities have the ability to undertake administrative acts implies providing them with measures to enforce orders and prohibitions arising directly from the provisions of law and administrative acts.[57] The initiation of administrative enforcement proceedings and the pursuit of enforcement actions are based on an enforceable title issued by the creditor and attached to the application or issued by an

[56] (Consolidated) Journal of Laws 2022, item 479; hereinafter AAEP.

[57] State authorities must have measures available to ensure that orders and prohibitions arising directly from provisions of law and from administrative acts are enforced – as it is pointed out – otherwise administration acts would be impossible - J. Olszanowski [in:] *Postępowanie administracyjne i sądowoadministracyjne*, eds. A. Hauser, A. Skoczylas, Warsaw 2021, p. 232.

enforcement authority that is the creditor, on the basis of which that authority commences enforcement *ex officio*.[58]

The competence of each police authority to act within the scope of enforcement authority, which refers to the administrative enforcement of obligations of a non-pecuniary nature indicated in cases defined by special provisions, was provided for by Article 20 § 2 of the Act on Administrative Enforcement Proceedings. The order to vacate immediately the jointly occupied dwelling and its immediate surroundings and the prohibition on approaching the jointly occupied dwelling and its immediate surroundings, which are indicated to a specified person on the basis of Article 15aa item 1 of the Police Act, are such an obligation of a non-pecuniary nature introduced by special provisions.

The competence of the police in terms of the possibility of taking action to compel compliance with a particular conduct is confirmed in Article 117 AAEP. It prescribes that police authorities, as enforcement authorities, may apply enforcement measures within the limits of their competence, which is determined as regards the imposition of obligations of a non-pecuniary nature in Article 20 § 2 AAEP. The Act on Administrative Enforcement Proceedings identifies possible enforcement measures depending on whether it is the enforcement of pecuniary performance or conduct not being the satisfaction of pecuniary performance. In the case of Article 117 AAEP, they were limited to the seizure of a thing, direct coercion and substitutive performance. Notably, these actions are undertaken without the need for issuing an enforceable title and serving an order on the application of an enforcement measure on the obliged party, which would be necessary in the absence of the provision of Article 117 AAEP.[59]

The possibility that the police take these actions is limited by a condition introduced in Article 117, which allows for such actions only when a delay in fulfilling the obligation would pose a threat to human life or health or serious damage to the national economy or when a special public interest so requires. As indicated above, the issuing of an order to vacate immediately the jointly occupied dwelling and its immediate surroundings and a prohibition on approaching the jointly occupied dwelling and its immediate surroundings (Article 15aa item 1 PA) takes place only when the perpetrator's conduct poses a threat to the life or health of household members (Article 15aa item 1 PA). Where the issue is human life or health, which are fundamental values, any degree of

[58] P. Przybysz, *Postępowanie egzekucyjne w administracji. Komentarz.* Warsaw 2021, pp. 218, 222-223.

[59] P. Przybysz, *Postępowanie egzekucyjne...*, p. 196.

threat is sufficient.[60] However, it is pointed out that in view of a limitation of procedural guarantees of parties to the proceedings in that way, these actions are applied in exceptional cases strictly regulated by law. The decision is to be based on the fact that a delay in performing the obligation implies a threat to goods that are particularly protected.[61] This empowerment extends to the actions involving the enforcement of directly given verbal commands. Accordingly, these measures are used for the enforcement of obligations arising either directly from a general provision or from an administrative decision, in addition to the verbal commands that have just been issued.[62]

The use of direct coercion is the most important of these measures. It consists of bringing about the performance of an enforceable obligation by the threat of use or by the use of directly effective measures. Such a measure may be the use of physical force to overcome the resistance of the obliged person and the resistance of other persons who stand in the way of the performance of the obligation (Article 148 § 1 AAEP).[63] Direct coercion can be used to cause the obliged person to perform the obligation to vacate the real estate, dwelling, surrender things, and also in those cases where, due to the nature of the obligation, it is not possible to apply other enforcement measures (Article 148 § 2 AAEP). Direct coercion may also be used immediately to perform the obligation arising from a provision of law, after a verbal command from an enforcement authority, without any prior reminder to the obliged person and without serving him/her with a copy of an enforceable title and of an order for performance of the obligation (Article 148 § 1 AAEP).

It should be reiterated that enforcement measures can be used under this simplified procedure in a situation of threat as the context for an action arising from the empowerment of an authority. Then, lower procedural guarantees apply compared to the ordinary enforcement proceedings, but the need to act swiftly in order to protect such an important good as human life and health makes it possible to exclude the

[60] See also W. Sawczyn, *Postępowanie egzekucyjne w administracji. Komentarz*. eds. R. Hauser, M. Wierzbowski, Warsaw 2024, marginal number 8 to Article117.

[61] J. Radwanowicz-Wanczewska [in:] *Ustawa o postępowaniu egzekucyjnym w administracji. Komentarz*, ed. D. Kijowski, Lex/el 2015, marginal number 3.2 to Article 117.

[62] J. Radwanowicz-Wanczewska [in:] *Ustawa...*, marginal number 3.1 to Article 117.

[63] J.P. Tarno [in:] W. Chruścielewski, J.P. Tarno, P. Dańczak, *Postępowanie administracyjne i postępowanie przed sądami administracyjnymi*, Warsaw 2018, p. 451.

application of all the provisions introduced in the Act on Administrative Enforcement Proceedings.[64]

Moreover, in the substantive area of enforcement actions taken by police authorities, there is no possibility of recovering the real estate, clearing the dwelling and other rooms (Article 1a point 12 indent 4 AAEP). However, the Act defines the action of clearing the dwelling as an enforcement measure leading to the removal of the obliged person from the occupied dwelling or room to surrender the cleared dwelling to the creditor. It also applies to the obligation to surrender the real estate for a defined period. The introduction of the purpose of surrendering the cleared dwelling to the creditor distinguishes that enforcement action from coercion leading to the vacation of dwelling. Police authorities are not enforcement bodies empowered to enforce an obligation of a non-pecuniary nature by using an enforcement measure in the form of clearing the dwelling. That enforcement action is not necessary for isolating the family members from the perpetrator of violence.

In the case of issuing an order to vacate immediately the jointly occupied dwelling and its immediate surroundings and a prohibition on approaching the jointly occupied dwelling and its immediate surroundings, it is important to cause the perpetrator to vacate the dwelling. The use of direct coercive measure by police officers (Article 148 § 2 AAEP) to cause the perpetrator of violence to vacate the dwelling will be sufficient to isolate the remaining family members immediately. The empowerment of the police provided for in the Act on Administrative Enforcement Proceedings to use direct coercive measures to take away things will, in turn, be sufficient to enforce on the perpetrator of violence the conduct of handing over the keys to the dwelling, which is an obligation arising directly from the Act (Article 148 § 2 AAEP in conjunction with Article 15ae item 6 PA).

This should also include the situation of the police carrying out enforcement proceedings by way of administrative enforcement proceedings and issuing an administrative act laying down a prohibition on approaching a person experiencing violence closer than a distance prescribed in metres or a prohibition on contact with a person experiencing domestic violence (Article 15aaa item 1 PA). Another situation to be included is the enforcement of the prohibition on entering the premises of a school, educational, care, artistic, sports facility or a workplace accompanied by a prohibition on the perpetrator's presence on those premises (Article 15aaa item 2 PA). The basis for issuing these prohibitions is the perpetrator's conduct posing a threat to the life or

[64] W. Sawczyn, *Postępowanie egzekucyjne...*, marginal number 1 to Article 117.

health of a person experiencing violence. Thus, there are grounds for allowing actions to be taken immediately – where necessary – to enforce the perpetrator's compliance with the obligations arising from the issued prohibitions, even though they will be obligations to refrain from an act with a possible removal of the perpetrator of violence beyond the distance of the prohibition on approaching the person identified in the prohibition or a removal from the premises on which the violent perpetrator stays. The possibility of using direct coercion together with physical force to remove the resistance of the obliged person will be an effective measure for the implementation of these obligations (Article 148 § 1 AAEP).

The above enforcement measures can be used also at a later date during the period covered by the prohibitions, i.e., for 14 days, unless a shorter period is given in connection with a subsequent decision to issue a prohibition on approach or a prohibition on entry, as prescribed by Article 15aab item 3 PA (after the issuing of an order to vacate the dwelling and a prohibition on approaching it).

Authors point to the implementation by the police of the order to vacate the dwelling and the prohibition on approaching it according to the provisions of the Act on Direct Coercive Measures and Firearms, which is to enable the application of direct coercive measures directly against a perpetrator of violence.[65]
The Police Act imposes on police officers the obligation to take steps to verify whether the perpetrator of violence complies with the provisions of an order to vacate the dwelling and a prohibition on approaching it, a prohibition on entry – entering the premises of a school, educational, care or artistic facility, sports facility or a workplace and staying on those premises when the person experiencing violence is present in those localities. A violation of these obligations is a commission of a petty offence (Article 66b § 1 points 1 and 2 of the Petty Offences Code.[66]) The same applies to the deliberate non-compliance with a prohibition on approaching the person experiencing domestic violence prescribed in metres or a prohibition on contacting the person experiencing domestic violence (Article 66b § 2 point 1 POC).

The application of coercion as an enforcement measure to enforce a violent person's obligation of conduct does not preclude the imposition of a penalty in criminal

---

[65] J. Jagieła, *Nakazanie przez Policję osobie stosującej przemoc w rodzinie opuszczenie wspólnie zajmowanego mieszkania i jego bezpośredniego otoczenia lub zakazanie zbliżania się do mieszkania i jego bezpośredniego otoczenia* [in:] *Symbolae Andreae Marciniak dedicatae*, eds. J Jagieła, R. Kulski, Warsaw 2022 , p. 323.

[66] Act of 20 May 1971; (Consolidated) Journal of Laws 2023, item 2119: hereinafter POC.

proceedings, petty offence cases or disciplinary proceedings concerning a failure to fulfil an obligation (Article 16 AAEP).[67]

[67] Zastosowanie środka egzekucyjnego nie stoi na przeszkodzie wymierzeniu kary w postępowaniu w sprawach o wykroczenia - R. Hauser, Z. Leoński, *Postępowanie egzekucyjne w administracji. Komentarz*, eds. R. Hauser, A. Skoczylas, Warsaw 2014, p. 106; P. Kledzik [in:] Postępowanie administracyjne, egzekucyjne i sądowoadministracyjne, ed. M. Wierzbowski, Warsaw 2022, p. 487. The argument is based on the different objectives to be served by criminal type liability and administrative enforcement. In the former case, it is repression, in the latter it is the performance of an obligation - R. Hauser, Z. Leoński *Postępowanie*, p. 107.

Chapter IV

Securing a claim for an obligation to vacate the dwelling or to prohibit approaching it and issue further prohibitions

A police-issued order to vacate the dwelling and a prohibition on approaching it will be immediately enforceable, but their legal force will expire after 14 days. The duration of the directive of conduct prescribed in an order to vacate the dwelling and a prohibition on approaching it, a prohibition on approach, a prohibition on contact or a prohibition on entry may be extended only on the basis of an order delivered by an ordinary court issued in the context of protection proceedings (Article 15ak item 1 PA).

The extension of protection by removing the perpetrator of violence from the household members can result only from issuing an order to secure a claim by an ordinary court in consequence of the initiation of civil proceedings by the person affected by violence. The special provision of Article 755[2] § 4 CCP empowers the court to provide security by extending the duration of a police-issued order to vacate the dwelling and a prohibition on approaching it, or a prohibition on approach, a prohibition on contact, a prohibition on entry (Article 755[2] § 1 CCP). The Code shortens the time for hearing such an application to 3 days. However, further provisions on protection proceedings have remained unchanged so that it is easier for a person affected by violence to obtain legal protection.

Setting the basic international standards, the Istanbul Convention (Article 53 items 1 and 2 of the Convention) introduced an obligation for its Parties to adopt domestic regulations ensuring maximum protection of victims of all forms of violence, in particular by issuing adequate protection orders in the ongoing proceedings, which shall be immediately enforceable and implemented as informally and rapidly as possible.[68]

Article 731[1] §1 CCP prescribes that an applicant may request an order on security if he/she substantiates the claim and a legal interest in granting the security. A legal interest in granting security exists when the lack of security will make it impossible or

[68] P. Wiktorska, *Procedury prawne związane z możliwościami odseparowania sprawcy przemocy domowej od osoby doświadczającej przemocy*, Prawo w działaniu Sprawy karne 2021, No. 45, p. 80.

seriously impede the enforcement of the ruling given in the case or will otherwise prevent or seriously impede the achievement of the purpose of the proceedings in the case (Article 730[1] § 2 CCP).

The security will consist of requiring the perpetrator of domestic violence to vacate the jointly occupied dwelling and its immediate surroundings or prohibiting that person from approaching the jointly occupied dwelling and its immediate surroundings when, by occupying the shared dwelling with other household members, he/she makes the co-occupation particularly burdensome by his/her conduct involving domestic violence (Article 11a item 1 ACDV).

Such a claim is secured by creating a situation that protects the applicant from violent actions for the duration of examination proceedings. Under the general provision of Article 731 CCP, a security may not seek to satisfy a claim, unless otherwise provided by law (Article 731 CCP). In the case of securing non-pecuniary claims, the court gives such security as it sees fit in the circumstances, without excluding the means provided for safeguarding pecuniary claims. The court may regulate the rights and obligations of the parties or participants in the proceedings for the duration of proceedings (Article 755 § 1 point 1 CCP). Notably, the Code introduces a special provision in the case of a claim involving protection from domestic violence. Under Article 755[2] § 1 CCP, the court may also grant security by extending the duration of an order to vacate immediately the jointly occupied dwelling and its immediate surroundings and a prohibition on approaching the jointly occupied dwelling and its immediate surroundings; a prohibition on approaching the person experiencing violence, a prohibition on contacting that person; a prohibition on entering the premises of a school, educational, care, artistic, sports facility attended by the person experiencing domestic violence or a workplace or any other locality in which that person habitually or regularly stays, accompanied by a prohibition on the perpetrator's presence on those premises. However, the grounds for the court's ruling obliging a perpetrator of violence to vacate the jointly occupied dwelling and its immediate surroundings or prohibiting the perpetrator from approaching the jointly occupied dwelling and its immediate surroundings differ from those applicable to a prohibition on approaching the person affected by violence, a prohibition on contacting that person; a prohibition issued in respect of the perpetrator of violence on entering the premises of a school, educational, care, artistic, sports facility attended by the person experiencing domestic violence or a workplace or any other locality in which that person habitually or regularly stays, accompanied by a prohibition on the perpetrator's presence on those premises (Article 11aa items 1,2,4 ACDV). In the first place, the extension of an order to vacate immediately the jointly occupied dwelling and its immediate surroundings and a prohibition on approaching the jointly occupied dwelling and its immediate surroundings will be presented.

Regardless of which police-issued decision is to be extended, a court order shall be given before the expiry of the decision. Reducing the time limit for considering the application to 3 days does not change the obligations of the person seeking security. The person seeking security bears the burden of substantiating the claim and legal interest in obtaining security. The person should therefore gather the relevant evidence before making an application, whereas, giving the court time to consider the application, the time for a court-issued order extending the order and prohibitions is 14 days.

The legislator did not choose to impose on the police the obligation to hand over immediately all documentation relating to their investigation at the request of the court by electronic means (even if it has to be processed into electronic form). It would facilitate the substantiation of public interest and, it seems, the claim itself.

In the application for security filed with the court, the claim is based on facts which relate to the particularly burdensome nature of the conduct of a participant in the proceedings bearing the hallmarks of domestic violence (Article 11a item 1 ACDV). In turn, to issue an order and a prohibition, it is necessary to establish the presence of a threat to the health and life of family members in that situation (Article 15aa item 1 PA). On each such occasion the prosecutor's obligation to decide whether to submit an application for security to the court is actualized. The police serve the prosecutor with a copy of the order and prohibition on vacating and approaching the dwelling (Article 15ad item 4 sentence 1 PA). The prosecutor shall therefore decide whether the protection of the rule of law, citizens' rights or the public interest (Article 7 CCP) requires submitting an application for securing a claim.

There is no provision to exempt the applicant from the need to substantiate their legal interest, even though an order to vacate the dwelling and a prohibition on approaching it have already been issued, as well as a prohibition on contact and a prohibition on entry, which in most cases would be a sufficient circumstance to substantiate it. However, as regards bringing certain claims, the legislator chose to exempt a party from the obligation to substantiate a claim, as is the case with a claim for maintenance (Article 753 § 1 CCP).

The court-issued order on security can relate to an extension of the duration of an order to vacate immediately the jointly occupied dwelling and its immediate surroundings and a prohibition on approaching the jointly occupied dwelling and its immediate surroundings. Extending the duration of an order to vacate and a prohibition on approaching the jointly occupied dwelling and its immediate surroundings in a court order on securing a claim, the court can modify the content of the above order and prohibition in terms of a prescribed area or a distance from the jointly occupied dwelling (Article 755^2 §1 sentence 2 CCP). The legislator did not provide for broader powers of the court when the court obliges the perpetrator of violence to vacate the dwelling or prohibits him/her from approaching it in its ruling on the request of an application. A police-issued decision relates to an order to vacate the dwelling and a prohibition on approaching it, by which the court is constrained in deciding whether to extend the duration of such an administrative act when the security does not burden the obliged party beyond what is necessary to ensure due protection for the eligible party (Article 730^1 § 3 CCP).

The above regulation of securing a claim by extending the duration of a police-issued order and prohibition should be seen as the satisfaction of the provisions of Article 53 of the Istanbul Convention by the legislator.[69] When deciding to grant such a security measure, the court specifies the frequency with which the police will verify whether the imposed order and prohibitions are not being breached, taking into account the provisions of Article 15ai item 1 of the Police Act. In the duration of an order and a prohibition, a prohibition on approach, a prohibition on contact or a prohibition on entry issued by the police, police officers verify at least three times whether a particular order or prohibition has been breached. The first check takes place the day after they are issued. In the event of their breach, the police take the necessary steps, which involves the possibility of enforcing the perpetrator's obligation using coercive measures and initiating petty offence proceedings.

Despite an extension of the duration of an order to vacate immediately the jointly occupied dwelling and its immediate surroundings and a prohibition on approaching the jointly occupied dwelling and its immediate surroundings, the steps taken by the police come down to the control of the non-violation of an order and a prohibition laid down in the administrative act, with their duration extended in an order on security. Should an order to vacate immediately the jointly occupied dwelling and its immediate surroundings and a prohibition on approaching the jointly occupied dwelling and its immediate surroundings be breached by re-entry of the perpetrator of violence into the dwelling, or if the order could not be complied with, the steps compelling the perpetrator of violence to vacate the dwelling could only be taken under the provisions on court enforcement proceedings. Enforcement cases fall within the competence of

[69] K. Flaga – Gieruszyńska [in:] *Kodeks postępowania cywilnego Postępowanie zabezpieczające*, ed. J. Gołaczyński, Warsaw 2021, pp. 234-235.

district courts and court enforcement officers attached to those courts (Article 758 CCP). However, the court enforcement officer does not have the power to use direct coercive measures to enforce such an obligation on a perpetrator of violence. It will be necessary to obtain police assistance to remove the resistance of the person obliged to vacate the dwelling (Article 765 § 1 CCP). The detailed rules for the possibility of carrying out enforcement actions by the police are specified in an implementing act.[70]

Under § 2 item 1 of the Regulation, the police provide assistance to a court enforcement officer in the performance of enforcement actions if, in the course of such actions, a court enforcement officer encounters resistance that hinders or prevents him/her from performing such actions or if there is a reasonable suspicion that such resistance may be encountered. In the event of a disruption of enforcement actions by participants in the proceedings, the police call on those persons – verbally – to behave in such a way as to enable the court enforcement officer to carry out enforcement actions (§ 2 item 2 of the Regulation). In the event where the participants in the proceedings fail to comply with the police-issued call as regards the conduct enabling the court enforcement officer to perform enforcement actions, the police will take steps in respect of them directed at the implementation of actions by the court enforcement officer. Unfortunately, these actions are not listed. Were they to be connected with direct coercion, they shall be provided for by statute. Nor is there in any basis for extending the application of Article 117 AAEP in this case, which was introduced as a special empowerment of the enforcement authority in administrative enforcement proceedings. One element taken by the legislator from the administrative procedure applied in consequence of issuing an order and prohibitions is, when they are extended, the need for the police to control the perpetrator's conduct, which involves concluding that a petty offence has been committed (Article 66b § 1 and 2 Petty Offences Code).

In the case of securing a claim for obliging a perpetrator of violence to vacate the jointly occupied dwelling and its immediate surroundings or prohibiting the perpetrator from approaching the jointly occupied dwelling and its immediate surroundings, Article 11a ACDV prescribes that the enforcement of the ruling is carried out under the provisions of the Code of Civil Procedure on the enforcement of the obligation to clear the dwelling serving a debtor's housing needs (Article 11a item 5 ACDV).

[70] The Regulation of the Minister of Internal Affairs and Administration on the provision of assistance to court enforcement officers by the Police or the Border Guard in carrying out enforcement actions of 15 March 2019 (Journal of Laws 2019, item 551).

Where an order on granting security is carried out by way of enforcement, the provisions on enforcement proceedings apply accordingly to the enforcement of that order (Article 743 § 1 CCP). An analysis of that procedure is given in Chapter V, but it is justified to point out now that the procedure will not allow for the swift enforcement of an order on security. Similarly, a prohibition on approaching the dwelling, despite an extension of its duration, will require enforcement action in the context of court enforcement proceedings, which may undermine the effects of the previous isolation of the perpetrator of violence from the household members.

It should be added that in the duration of an order and a prohibition, the police verify whether the order or prohibition, the validity of which has been extended by the court in an order on security, is not being breached and take the necessary measures (Article 755^2 § 2 CCP taking into account Article 15ai item 1 PA). A breach of an order to vacate immediately the jointly occupied dwelling and its immediate surroundings or a prohibition on approaching the jointly occupied dwelling and its immediate surroundings laid down in a court order on granting security in cases relating to obliging a perpetrator of family violence to vacate the jointly occupied dwelling and its immediate surroundings or prohibiting that person from approaching the jointly occupied dwelling and its immediate surroundings is a petty offence punishable by a penalty of imprisonment, limitation of liberty or a fine (Article 66b § 1 and 2 Petty Offences Code).

Chapter V

Court civil procedure as a basis for protection from violence

5.1. Request of an application

A separate procedure before ordinary courts is the cornerstone of protection for counteracting domestic violence introduced into the legal order of the Republic of Poland. The rules for the operation of this procedure were introduced in Division IA of the Code of Civil Procedure: Cases within the scope of counteracting domestic violence.

Article 29 of the Istanbul Convention introduces the obligation to ensure victims of any form of violence covered by its scope adequate civil remedies against the perpetrator within the domestic legal system.[71] The provisions of this chapter of the Code aim to allow for a swift and efficient conduct of examination proceedings and delivery of a ruling by the court upon application of a person experiencing domestic violence. The person seeks such protection in court proceedings requiring that the perpetrator of domestic violence be obliged to vacate the jointly occupied dwelling and its immediate surroundings or prohibited from approaching the dwelling and its immediate surroundings (Article 11a item 1 ACDV). The request applies to any dwelling serving current housing needs (Article 11a item 4 ACDV).

The operation of the courts is the administration of justice, which consists, among other things, of adjudicating legal conflicts or non-conflicting cases in the sphere of fundamental rights and civic freedoms.[72] It will be carried out by establishing legal consequences on the basis of applicable legal rules in a way that is binding and firm for the designated actors.[73] The adjudication of such conflicts must be imperative in nature, which is embodied, where applicable, in the sanction as the possibility of the

---

[71] S. Spurek, *Nasza Konwencja...*, p.197. Article 29 item 1 of the Convention prescribes that Parties shall take the necessary legislative or other measures to provide victims with adequate civil remedies against the perpetrator.

[72] K. Lubiński., *Pojęcie i zakres wymiaru sprawiedliwości*, Studia Prawnicze 1987, No. 4, p. 24.

[73] K. Lubiński, *Pojęcie i zakres...*, p. 16.

coercive enforcement of a ruling by means of the coercive measures provided for by law or in the enforcement of a ruling in a manner corresponding to its content.[74]

Compared to the short-term police-issued administrative act, the court-issued order obliging the perpetrator to vacate the dwelling and the immediate surroundings or prohibiting that person from approaching the dwelling and the immediate surroundings will continue to provide protection from violence. A court ruling is immediately enforceable, giving protection from acts of violence, provided that the legal proceedings are swift and efficient.[75] Such proceedings do not breach the right to defence of the perpetrator of violence and the requirements of a fair and impartial trial.[76] They are not dependent on the initiation of other court proceedings, such as criminal proceedings or proceedings for the dissolution of marriage. The conduct of other criminal or civil proceedings involving protection from domestic violence against the same perpetrator shall not be an obstacle to the issuing of an order obliging the perpetrator to vacate the dwelling or prohibiting the perpetrator from approaching the dwelling and the immediate surroundings.[77] The envisaged regulations are an implementation of the obligation under Article 53 items 1 and 2 of the Istanbul Convention. Moreover, in May 2023, the Council of the European Union adopted two decisions on a draft concerning being bound by the Istanbul Convention. On 10 May 2023, the European Parliament has consented to binding the European Union by the Convention in relation to institutions and public administration (separately for matters related to judicial cooperation in criminal matters, asylum and non-refoulement). On 1 June 2023, the Council of the European Union adopted a decision (2023/1075) on the conclusion, on behalf of the European Union, of the Council of Europe Convention on preventing and combating violence against women and domestic violence with regard to institutions and public administration of the Union. A further part of the decision provides that the Union's accession to the Convention as regards matters falling within its exclusive competence is without prejudice to the Member States' competence as regards the ratification of the Convention on matters falling within their national competences. The European Union adopted an international agreement binding itself by the provisions of the Convention to the extent of the above declaration, which will strengthen Member States in the implementation of its provisions.

---

[74] K. Lubiński, *Pojęcie i zakres...*, pp. 16-17.

[75] See S. Spurek, *Nasza Konwencja...* p. 239.

[76] S. Spurek, *Nasza Konwencja..*, p. 240.

[77] S. Spurek, *Nasza Konwencja..*, p. 241.

A person experiencing violence can also require that the court issue a prohibition against the perpetrator on approaching that person at a distance expressed in metres if the perpetrator's conduct involving the use of domestic violence poses a threat to the life or health of the person experiencing violence (Article 11aa item 1 ACDV). The person can also require that the perpetrator of domestic violence be prohibited from contacting him/her. The request to prohibit the perpetrator of domestic violence from contacting him/her also applies to the situation of harassing that person by means of remote electronic communication, arousing a sense of threat, humiliation, anguish justified by the circumstances or substantially invading his/her privacy (Article 11aa item 2 ACDV). When attending school, an educational, care or artistic facility, doing sport or performing work, a person experiencing violence can require that the court issue, in a situation where the perpetrator's conduct poses a threat to his/her life or health, a prohibition in respect of the perpetrator of violence on entering the premises of a school, educational, care, artistic, sports facility attended by the person experiencing domestic violence or a workplace or any other locality in which that person habitually or regularly stays, accompanied by a prohibition on the perpetrator's presence on those premises (Article 11aa item 4 ACDV). The above requests for legal protection regarding the issuing of a prohibition on approach, a prohibition on contact or a prohibition on entry were introduced into the Act on Counteracting Domestic Violence by means of a law of 13 January 2023.[78]

To begin court proceedings, which can be initiated only upon application (Article 506 CCP), a person experiencing violence submits an adequate letter – an application (Article 511 § 1 CCP). It will include a request that the court issue an order obliging the perpetrator of violence to vacate the jointly occupied dwelling and its immediate surroundings or to cease to approach the dwelling and its immediate surroundings (Article 11a item 1 ACDV). The provision of Article 11a item 1 ACDV introduces a basis for such an application. It is a situation in which a perpetrator of domestic violence occupies a dwelling jointly with a person experiencing violence and the co-occupation is particularly burdensome because of the perpetrator's conduct. The situations that constitute domestic violence are defined in Article 2 item 1 point 1 letters a-e ACDV. Particular burdensomeness will be associated with conduct which, displayed on a single occasion with considerable force of such violence, makes the co-occupation particularly burdensome. It will also be repetitive conduct, which falls within the category of violence despite the absence of such singular force of action and makes the co-occupation particularly burdensome because of its recurrence. Not every case of the perpetrator's conduct carrying the risk for the life or health of the household

[78] See footnote 6.

members – including a single incident – will be the basis for filing an application for a court to issue an order obliging the perpetrator to vacate the dwelling and prohibiting that perpetrator from approaching it.

Domestic violence must lead to particular burdensomeness as regards co-occupation. Both terms are imprecise leaving it up to the court to decide whether to classify the conduct identified during the evidence proceedings as particularly burdensome. The type of violence the perpetrator resorts to is significant. It must take such a form that the effect it produces makes co-occupation particularly burdensome. The mere necessity of living with a person who is unkind, unfriendly, hostile, negative, and does not cooperate in the joint maintenance of the property is burdensome, but it need not necessarily be particularly burdensome.[79]

The provision of Article 11aa item 2 points 1-3 ACDV complements situations involving the use of domestic violence when a direct interpretation of the provision of Article 11a ACDV did not allow for delivering a ruling as to protection from domestic violence before the amendment of 13 January 2023.

There is no doubt about the situation of providing legal protection to a person experiencing violence in the form of issuing an order obliging the perpetrator of violence to vacate the jointly occupied dwelling and its immediate surroundings or prohibiting the perpetrator from approaching the dwelling and its immediate surroundings if the person experiencing domestic violence has vacated the jointly occupied dwelling because of the violence he/she suffered in the dwelling (Article 11a item 2 point 1 ACDV). The adequate legal protection would be missing if a person running away from violence lost such protection. Otherwise that person would be exposed to conduct bearing the hallmarks of violence only to be able to require that its perpetrator vacate the dwelling. As it was rightly formulated in literature: "Provisions are issued not in order to give expression to the *apriori*, even most logical theoretical constructions, but to meet certain real practical needs, to regulate certain issues that are actually present in the practice of social and legal life."[80]

The legislator gives a person experiencing violence the possibility of submitting a request to oblige the perpetrator to vacate the jointly occupied dwelling and its immediate surroundings or to prohibit the perpetrator from approaching the dwelling and its immediate surroundings (Article 11a item 2 point 2 ACDV) even though the

---

[79] Order of the Regional Court of 24 August 2023, III Ca 549/23, Lex No. 3654352.

[80] J. Jodłowski, *Kilka kwestii z teorii międzynarodowego postępowania cywilnego*, PiP 1974, No. 2, p. 102.

perpetrator of domestic violence has vacated the jointly occupied dwelling. It is not a case of temporary absence from the dwelling due to personal or professional matters, a stay in another locality as a result of a business trip or for health reasons. It is supported by taking into account the objective introduced by the Act on Counteracting Domestic Violence to isolate the perpetrator of violence from the household members to eliminate a situation where further acts of violence could occur. Vacating the dwelling by the perpetrator is not equivalent to moving out of the dwelling when that person takes all his/her belongings, communicating that fact to the party from whom he/she derives the right to the dwelling. The court-issued ruling relates to vacating the dwelling to remove a situation allowing the perpetrator to continue acts of violence that make the occupation of dwelling particularly burdensome. Vacating the dwelling as temporary non-use does not imply the abandonment of the will to re-enter it. The court's decision obliging the perpetrator to vacate the dwelling does not include an obligation to clear it by taking all belongings with the obligation to hand it over to an authorised person, but merely to vacate the dwelling to eliminate further acts of violence.

The ruling will not be given once it has been established that the perpetrator of violence has lost his/her right to the dwelling when one of the obligations of that person is to vacate the dwelling. A ruling issued in a situation where there is no right to the dwelling would entail a final ruling excluding the possibility of further use of dwelling, returning to it or undertaking other actions relating to the dwelling, which will be possible in the event of a change in the situation giving rise to the ruling issued based on the Act of Counteracting Domestic Violence.[81] The court’s order obliging the perpetrator to vacate the dwelling is a command regarding conduct, which will amount to the exclusion of the use of dwelling for residential purposes by the perpetrator of violence.

In turn, moving out of the dwelling will be another case of requiring that the court issue an order for vacating the jointly occupied dwelling and its immediate surroundings or prohibit the perpetrator of violence from approaching the dwelling and its immediate surroundings periodically or intermittently occupied together with the person experiencing domestic violence (Article 11a item 2 point 3 ACDV).

The hypothesis of the standard that requires the vacation of dwelling will be fulfilled by the fact of occasional use of dwelling. It is the case when a perpetrator of violence stays in one dwelling and, in addition, still uses the dwelling occupied by the person experiencing violence. The introduction of a special provision makes it possible to qualify such occasional stay in the dwelling as occupancy, without regard to the

---

[81] See point 5.4.

assessment of the situation as staying in the dwelling and, above all, as an intention to reside there permanently. It is a case of vacating the dwelling while living in another locality, when that person no longer remains in the dwelling where acts of violence occurred. However, a situation occurs where a perpetrator of violence visits the dwelling with the intention of staying there irregularly or periodically, using the dwelling to that extent, though without wishing to reside there permanently as the second element of the concept of domicile (Article 25 Civil Code[82]).

The issue of future occupancy of dwelling based on a legal title held will have no impact on the assessment of such stay, which the court does not take into account in its findings of fact. Accordingly, in the event of vacating the dwelling and taking one's personal belongings, which results in a transfer of the perpetrator's place of residence to another accommodation, it will no longer be well-founded to deliver a decision including a command regarding conduct in the form of vacating the dwelling. Nonetheless, the factual state may support the need to issue a prohibition on approaching the dwelling. It is not possible to exclude cases when the manifestations of violence took place both in the dwelling and its immediate surroundings, where the victim, for example, works, goes shopping, attends classes or carries out physical activities. It is regardless of the possibility of issuing also a prohibition on entry, when the facts connected with violence posing a threat to that person's life or health have already taken place and point to the possibility of the perpetrator's re-entry into such localities, which are at a considerable distance from the premises (Article 11aa item 4 ACDV). It will be a prohibition issued in respect of the perpetrator of violence on entering the premises of a school, educational, care, artistic, sports facility attended by the person experiencing domestic violence or a workplace or any other locality in which that person habitually or regularly stays, accompanied by a prohibition on the perpetrator's presence on those premises (Article 11aa item 4 ACDV).

The obligation to vacate the dwelling or the prohibition on approach applies also to their surroundings because the perpetrator of violence can continue to occupy outbuildings, cellars, workshops, garages that are adjacent to the dwelling.[83]
Taking into consideration of the function of civil procedure to establish and give effect to individual and specific legal norms in the area of civil law, family and guardianship law, labour law[84] entails the need to designate this conduct properly in the court's

[82] Under the definition of domicile load down in Article 25 of the Civil Code, it is the place where a natural person stays with the intention of residing permanently.

[83] P. Wiktorska, *Procedury prawne...*, p. 86.

[84] K. Markiewicz, *Zasady orzekania w postępowaniu nieprocesowym*, Warszawa 2013, p. 13 and the views of science quoted there.

decision using a statutory expression: the dwelling and its immediate surroundings. Therefore, the legislator clarified the court's decision further. In the issued order obliging the perpetrator of violence to vacate the jointly occupied dwelling and its immediate surroundings or prohibiting the perpetrator from approaching the jointly occupied dwelling and its immediate surroundings, the court defines the area that a perpetrator of domestic violence must vacate and cannot enter or the distance from the jointly occupied dwelling which the perpetrator is required to keep (Article 560^7 §1).

These terms have not been defined. It was only indicated in Article 560^7 § 1 CCP that the court is obliged to define the area or distance from the jointly occupied dwelling to be kept by the perpetrator of violence. Nevertheless, it is necessary to set a precise directive of conduct for the participant in the proceedings, whether it is a descriptive designation of the area to be vacated or the distance to be kept.

When an interpreter seeks to achieve the objective of the text of a law[85] as a guarantee of the most comprehensive protection from domestic violence, it is appropriate to attribute to the text in question the meaning that is the most complete means of achieving the objective.[86] The objective will be achieved when a participant in the proceedings is obliged to vacate the jointly occupied dwelling and its immediate surroundings, understood as an obligation to vacate the dwelling together with the rooms or land closely connected to the dwelling. In the case of a prohibition on approaching the dwelling and its immediate surroundings, the court also defines, in addition to the area in the above meaning, the area or distance from the jointly occupied dwelling that the perpetrator of domestic violence will be obliged to keep. The perpetrator will be forced to refrain from breaching an area or distance prescribed in a descriptive manner or in a unit of measurement. The introduction of a standard of conduct as a prohibition will not be a singular conduct but a continuous obligation in the form of refraining from an action consisting of crossing the boundary set for the participant. Both the order to vacate the dwelling and the prohibition on approaching the dwelling in connection with specific acts referring to the conduct of a perpetrator of violence will result in the achievement of the objectives of the law. In this way the disposition of a legal standard relating to the situation of the use of family violence is alternative, the court may oblige the perpetrator of domestic violence only to vacate the jointly occupied dwelling and its immediate surroundings. It may also deliver an order obliging the perpetrator to vacate the dwelling and prohibiting the perpetrator from approaching it.

---

[85] T. Gizbert – Studnicki, *Wykładnia celowościowa*, Studia Prawnicze 1985, manuscript 3-4, p. 54.
[86] T. Gizbert – Studnicki, *Wykładnia celowościowa…*, p. 60.

Another issue arising in the course of examination proceedings, which is relevant to the decision obliging a perpetrator to vacate the dwelling, is to establish the right to occupy the dwelling. The legislator provided that it would not be relevant in a case of counteracting domestic violence. For the purposes of deciding the case, neither the right to occupy the dwelling held by a person submitting an application for a ruling obliging the perpetrator of violence to vacate the dwelling nor the perpetrator's legal title to possess and use the dwelling are subject to examination. An obligation to vacate the dwelling will also be imposed on a perpetrator with an exclusive right to the dwelling, including the right of ownership. In that case, the obligation to vacate the dwelling is independent of who owns it or what legal title the perpetrator of violence has to it. On the other hand, the perpetrator may continue to dispose of his/her right to the dwelling by selling or renting it.[87] The request for a court ruling involves obliging the perpetrator of violence only to vacate the dwelling with no possibility of return until such an order has been modified (Article 560^7 § 5 sentence 2 CCP).

A court ruling on the loss of the right to the dwelling by a perpetrator of violence is not relevant either. The perpetrator will be able to take steps to use and reside in the dwelling again, though it will be necessary to initiate further court proceedings, such as proceedings on the dissolution of marriage. In turn, in the event where an action is brought for clearing the dwelling by persons residing in it, with a prior civil law act terminating the legal relationship arising from their occupation of dwelling – normally in relation to lending of dwelling free of charge – its validity will be examined in terms of the incompatibility of the claim with the principles of social coexistence (Article 5 Civil Code). Alternatively, a judgement will set a date for clearing the dwelling, allowing household members to find another accommodation (Article 320 CCP). The obligation to vacate the dwelling and its immediate surroundings issued by the court based on Article 11a item 1 ACDV does not provide for the duration of the obligation. In turn, under Article 560^7 § 5 CCP, this order may be repealed or modified as a result of a change in the circumstances of the case, even if it were contested or final. An application submitted by a perpetrator of violence to modify an order obliging that perpetrator to vacate the dwelling and preventing him/her from using it will be based only on circumstances relating to a change in the situation within the scope of possible actions bearing the hallmarks of violence.[88]

Specific regulations have been introduced in the area of legal protection of individuals experiencing domestic violence to ensure such protection in the form of submitting an

[87] P. Wiktorska, *Procedury prawne*…, p. 84; J. Jagieła, *Nakazanie*..., p. 321.

[88] See more point 5.4.

application for obliging the perpetrator of violence to vacate the jointly occupied dwelling and its immediate surroundings or prohibiting the perpetrator from approaching the dwelling and its immediate surroundings. A person experiencing violence is not deprived of the possibility of taking steps that will also lead to gaining protection from the perpetrator of violence, though through other court proceedings. The Act on the Protection of Tenants' Rights[89] makes it possible to make a request for evicting a spouse, divorced spouse or other cohabitant of the same dwelling from the dwelling if the latter's grossly reprehensible conduct makes co-occupation impossible (Article 13 item 2 APTR). In that case, the legislator introduces the term of request as a court-ordered eviction of the respondent. The legislator does not make use of the term "clear the dwelling," as it is with other cases listed in the Act, where a party wishes to regain the possibility of using or disposing of dwelling. Although the legislator introduces the word "eviction" into the content of the provision, the directive regarding the respondent's conduct should be assumed to mean the order to clear the dwelling, as is the case with the other provisions of the Act. As a result of granting the claim, after examination proceedings have been held in the form of trial, a judgement obliging the perpetrator to vacate, clear and surrender the dwelling (place it at the disposal of an authorised person) is delivered. In a judgement obliging the perpetrator to clear the dwelling (whose content also includes the obligation to vacate the dwelling and surrender it), the court rules on the right to enter into an agreement for the lease of social housing or the lack of such right of the individuals covered by the order. The obligation to provide a lease for social housing rests on the commune with jurisdiction over the location of the dwelling to be cleared (Article 14 item 1 APTR). However, such entitlement is not be ordered by a court where family violence is the reason for clearing the dwelling (Article 17 item 1 APTR), which covers domestic violence (in the absence of an adjustment of this expression to the amendments to the Act on Counteracting Domestic Violence).

Similarly, the regulation laid down in Article 16 APTR, which excludes the admissibility of enforcement of a judgment ordering the clearing of dwelling between 1 November and 31 March of the following year inclusive if the evicted person has not been indicated another dwelling to which the re-housing could take place, is also not applicable to a judgment ordering the clearing of dwelling due to the use of domestic violence.

In the event of a judgment dissolving a marriage, in exceptional cases, where the grossly reprehensible conduct of one of the spouses makes cohabitation impossible, the

---

[89] See footnote 40.

court may order an eviction of that person at the request of the other spouse (Article 58 § 2 sentence 2 Family and Guardianship Code[90]).

5.2. The course of court proceedings

The request submitted by a person experiencing domestic violence is examined pursuant to the provisions of the Code of Civil Procedure. The Code regulates court proceedings in, *inter alia*, civil law relationships (Article 1 CCP). The legislator chose to carry out examination proceedings in the case of a request based on the protection of household members from acts of violence under the rules of non-contentious proceedings, additionally introducing specific provisions into Articles 560^2 – 560^{12} CCP.

Notably, the legislator chose to limit examination proceedings, the subject-matter of which consists only of statements of facts proving the existence of domestic violence. Nonetheless, it is necessary to carry out evidence proceedings to establish such facts. Difficulties are generally due to limited evidence because the events typically take place in the dwelling in the absence of third persons as witnesses. These facts will largely be established based on the use of the institute of factual presumption.[91]

Given the special nature of those proceedings, it is acknowledged that a public prosecutor should participate in them. The public prosecutor is not a participant in these proceedings *ex officio*. The prosecutor must only be served a copy of the application and copies of judicial writs with a notice of hearing, as prescribed by Article 560^4 § 2 CCP.[92]
The service of a copy of the application and a notice of hearing on the public prosecutor will make it possible, based on the information obtained in those proceedings, to initiate adequate criminal proceedings against the perpetrator of domestic violence for an act prosecuted by public indictment. The prosecutor may thus get familiar with other ongoing criminal proceedings against the perpetrator of violence, which may be relevant to the ruling on a civil case.[93]

---

[90] Act of 25 February 1964 (Consolidated) Journal of Laws 2023, item 2809; hereinafter FGC.

[91] Under Article 231 CCP, the court may accept facts relevant to the outcome of the case as established if such a conclusion may be inferred from other established facts.

[92] P. Woś, *Postępowanie wobec osoby stosującej przemoc w rodzinie w Kodeksie postępowania cywilnego*, Studia Prawnicze KUL 2023, No. 1, p. 134.

[93] A. Laskowska – Hulisz, *Postępowanie nieprocesowe w sprawach o zobowiązanie osoby stosującej przemoc w rodzinie do opuszczenia wspólnie zajmowanego mieszkania i jego bezpośredniego*

Based on general provisions – Article 55 sentence 1 in conjunction with Article 7 and Article 13 § 2 CCP – proceedings obliging a perpetrator of violence to vacate the dwelling or prohibiting the perpetrator from approaching it, prohibiting the perpetrator from harassment or entry may be initiated by a public prosecutor. The prosecutor is also entitled to join ongoing proceedings based on Article 60 § 1 in conjunction with Article 13 § 2 CCP at their every stage and participate in them.[94]

An analysis of court cases relating to obliging a perpetrator of violence to vacate the dwelling or prohibiting a perpetrator from approaching it was presented in a scientific study. The study covered the files of 192 cases concluded by a final and binding ruling in 34 district courts randomly selected from entire Poland.[95] In 160 examined cases, the court adjourned the first scheduled hearing in as many as 75 cases, which is 46.90%. The most common reasons for adjournment involved the failure to serve the summons for a hearing on the participants in the proceedings properly or the necessity to continue the evidence proceedings (by taking evidence through questioning witnesses) – which applied to 30 adjourned cases (24.6% of the causes of adjournment).[96]

The court issues a ruling on the request of an application having carried out examination proceedings with the obligation to schedule a hearing for the taking of evidence (Article 560^4 § 1 CCP), and it informs a public prosecutor of its date (Article 560^4 § 2 sentence 2 CCP). The decision is to be made within 1 month from the date of receipt of the application by the court (Article 560^5 CCP). To ensure expeditious proceedings, when it is simultaneously indispensable, the court may carry out the service using the police (Article 560^6 § 1 CCP). In that case, separate procedural rules were introduced for effecting the service by the police (Article 560^6 § 2-4 CCP). Although the provisions of Article 560^6 CCP allow for including the police in the service of judicial letters, it does not seem that this measure truly allows proceedings to be expedited without infringing on the participant's right to the court. The police are to take steps to effect service within 7 days of being assigned the task and even to find, if the addressee is not present, whether he/she resides at the address for service (Article

---

otoczenia lub zakazanie zbliżania się do mieszkania i jego bezpośredniego otoczenia, *Komentarz*, Lex/el 2020, comment 10.

[94] A. Kiełtyka, A. Ważny, *Przeciwdziałanie przemocy w rodzinie. Komentarz*, A. Kiełtyka, A. Ważny, Warsaw 2015, p. 194.

[95] F. Manikowski, *Postępowanie w sprawie o zobowiązania osoby stosującej przemoc w rodzinie do opuszczenia wspólnie zajmowanego mieszkania i jego bezpośredniego otoczenia lub zakazania zbliżania się do mieszkania i jego bezpośredniego otoczenia - analiza badań aktowych*, Prawo w działaniu. Sprawy cywilne, 2022, No. 50, p. 11.

[96] F. Manikowski, *Postępowanie…*, p. 22.

560^{6} § 2 and 3 CCP). A positive finding allows for leaving a notification of the possibility of receipt of the letter in the court that is hearing the case within 7 days of placing the notification (Article 560^{6} § 4 CCP). It is in conflict with the content of the general provision of Article 139 § 1 CCP, which introduces an obligation to notify the addressee twice about a delivery left at the postal operator's outlet with a deadline of 7 days for its collection. The police must also establish the fact of the addressee's dwelling, which in the case of a participant in the proceedings, who has been ordered to vacate the dwelling and prohibited from approaching it, will make it impossible to become aware of the notification and collect the letter.

The court will rule on the application after the hearing is closed, taking as a basis the state of affairs existing at the time of the hearing (Article 316 § 1 in conjunction with Article 13 § 2 CCP). Participants may lodge an appeal against the order within two weeks of receipt of the reasoned order (Article 369 § 1 in conjunction with Article 13 § 2 CCP) as a result of an application submitted by the applicant within a week of delivery of the order (Article 560^{9} § 2 CCP). The initiated appeal proceedings mean that the case will be heard within the limits of appeal (Article 378 § 1 in conjunction with Article 13 § 2 CCP). The court of second instance will decide on the basis of the material gathered in an order delivered by the court of first instance and in the appeal proceedings (Article 382 CCP). A ruling shall be given by the court of second instance within one month of receiving the case file (Article 560^{12} CCP).

5.3. Surrender of things

In view of the possibility of a court ruling obliging a participant in the proceedings to vacate the jointly occupied dwelling and its immediate surroundings, as a person in respect of whom such an application was submitted, or prohibiting that person from approaching the jointly occupied dwelling and its immediate surroundings – when it entails the need for taking immediate steps to prevent acts of violence by means of an order on securing a claim – a participant is entitled to submit an application for permission to recover items from the jointly occupied dwelling (Article 560^{3a} § 1 CCP).

The subject-matter of such an application submitted in the course of examination proceedings will be a request that the court permits the applicant to recover personal effects, items necessary for personal gainful employment, or pets owned by the perpetrator of violence, and necessary for daily living or gainful employment from the jointly occupied dwelling and its immediate surroundings (Article 560^{3a} § 1 CCP). The application entails court authorization to recover items from the jointly occupied dwelling if the person affected by violence does not consent to their surrender (Article 560^{3a} § 1 CCP).

In that regard, the legislator introduces separate incidental proceedings. A separate application is needed for their initiation. A participant shall specify his/her request by marking specific things such as personal effects, items necessary for personal gainful employment, or pets owned by the perpetrator of violence, and necessary for daily living or gainful employment, from the jointly occupied dwelling and its immediate surroundings. The application shall substantiate the use of the said things or the ownership of the animal and its indispensability for daily living or gainful employment (Article 560^{3a} § 2 CCP).

An application shall be examined immediately after its receipt. The Act leaves it to the discretion of the court to set a hearing to undertake fact-finding actions that form the basis of the decision, though the absence of the need for setting a hearing will be primarily connected with the conduct of the person affected by violence. This is because provision has been made for hearing explanations from the initiator of main proceedings mainly on protection from acts bearing the hallmarks of violence. The initiator can be informed about a participant's request for items by telephone or e-mail (provided that a telephone number or e-mail address has been given). This is also the way in which he/she may be informed about the permissible means of making explanations (Article 560^{3a} § 3 CCP). The lack of such explanations shall not be an obstacle to the issuing of a ruling, but the court shall base its decision on the statements included in the application and the measures substantiating the request (Article 560^{3a} § 4 CCP). The proceedings do not lead to a decision on the ownership of those items, as provided for in Article 560^{3a} § 6 sentence 2 CCP.

A complaint may be made in respect of a court-issued order to another panel of the court of first instance, so-called "horizontal complaint" (Article 560^{3a} § 7 CCP). A complaint is brought within a week from the date of service of the reasoned order as a result of an application for a statement of reasons and service of a copy of the reasoned order. The court serves *ex officio* only a copy of an order delivered in closed session (Article 357 § 2 sentence 1 CCP). Where, in making an order, the court refrained from giving a substantiation, pursuant to Article 357 § 6 CCP, the period within which a complaint may be brought shall start to run on the date of delivery of the order or, if it has been served, on the date of its service (Article 394 § 2 sentence 2 CCP in conjunction with Article 394^{1a} § 2 CCP).

In addition to the general procedural requirements defined in Article 126 CCP, a complaint as a judicial writ shall identify the order under appeal and propose that it be modified or repealed and state briefly the grounds of the complaint, if necessary setting out new facts and evidence (Article 394 § 3 in conjunction with Article 394^{1a} § 2 CCP). The court examines a complaint in a panel consisting of three judges (Article 394^{1a} § 1^2 CCP). The legislator provided that an order is effective and enforceable upon its delivery, despite the fact that such regulation follows from Article 360 CCP.[97] It does not seem that the legislator viewed the delivery of such an order as a ruling as to substance.

Provision is also made for an appropriate procedure for the enforcement of the ruling in the form of recovery of items, which is to take place in the presence of the police, after a date of recovery has been agreed with the person experiencing violence (Article 560^{3a} § 8 CCP). Should it be impossible to recover the items in this manner, the order will be subject to judicial enforcement carried out by means of non-pecuniary enforcement involving the surrender of movable property (Article 560^{3a} § 9 CCP). In the event where a complaint is lodged, the applicant will be able to require that enforcement of the contested order be suspended pending resolution of the complaint (Article 396 CCP).

Notably, the legislator envisaged the possibility of recover items from the dwelling already at the time when the police issue an administrative act in the form of an order to vacate the dwelling and a prohibition on approaching it. A person who has been ordered to vacate the dwelling and prohibited from approaching it has the right to recover personal effects, items necessary for personal gainful employment, or pets owned by the perpetrator of violence, and necessary for daily living or gainful employment from the jointly occupied dwelling and its immediate surroundings (Article 15ae item 4 sentence 1 PA). However, the exercise of this right was made conditional on the absence of objection from the person experiencing violence (Article 15ae item 4 sentence 2 PA). When an objection is raised, the items or domestic animals are left in the jointly occupied dwelling or its immediate surroundings with the possibility of bringing a civil action for surrender of those items (Article 15ae item 4 sentences 2 and 3 PA).

The right of a person obliged to vacate the dwelling to recover items from the dwelling has been extended during the period of validity of an administrative order and a

[97] Under Article 360 CCP, orders become effective to such an extent and in such a manner as is apparent from their contents upon their delivery or, if there has been no delivery, from the time their operative part is signed.

prohibition. When the need arises for a perpetrator of domestic violence to take personal effects, items necessary for personal gainful employment, or pets owned by the perpetrator of violence, and necessary for daily living or gainful employment from the jointly occupied dwelling and its immediate surroundings, the perpetrator can undertake such actions only once in the presence of a police officer (Article 15ae item 5 sentence 1 PA). These provisions do not make that possibility dependent on a lack of objection from the person experiencing violence, they only introduce the obligation to notify that person of the date on which the action is to take place, allowing him/her to take part in it (Article 15ae item 5 sentence 2 PA). However, the legislator provided that the recovery of such items can take place only when there is a need to recover property belonging to the perpetrator of violence from the jointly occupied dwelling and its immediate vicinity, particularly items previously not recovered. The creation of a standard authorising an action, when the provision of Article 15ae item 5 PA is introduced in the context of additional grounds for recovering items, leads to the conclusion that in this case, too, the objection of the person experiencing violence will exclude the admissibility of recovering items from the dwelling. It is particularly true if court proceedings on the surrender of things were taking place based on the provisions of civil substantive law, which is envisaged by Article 15ae item 4 sentence 3 PA, because such an action against the will of the person experiencing violence would circumvent the need for proceedings for the surrender of things.

Moreover, should the need arise to protect the animals being the property of a perpetrator of violence in respect of whom an order and a prohibition has been issued, the steps envisaged in the Act on the Protection of Animals shall be taken.[98] It will normally consist of taking the animal to an animal shelter (Article 7 item 1 point 1 APA) or taking further steps to protect such animals pursuant to Article 7 item 1 points 2 and 3 APA).

The need to use items that were in the dwelling appears also when the court delivers an order as to substance. In an order obliging a perpetrator of violence to vacate the jointly occupied dwelling and its immediate surroundings or prohibiting the perpetrator from approaching the jointly occupied dwelling and its immediate surroundings, the court may grant a temporary right to use the items in the jointly occupied dwelling or in its immediate surroundings (at the request submitted by an applicant or a participant in the proceedings) and define the manner of their use, provided that it does not cause undue delay in the proceedings. In the order, the court shall specify the date and manner

[98] Act of 21 August 1997 on the Protection of Animals, (Consolidated) Journal of Laws 2023, item 1580; hereinafter: APA.

of surrender of the things granted for use and, where appropriate, the period of their use. The provisions on the recovery of items in the presence of the police at a time agreed with the person experiencing violence shall apply accordingly to the enforcement of the order granting the right to use things, of which adequate minutes shall be drawn up (Article 560^{3a} § 8 CCP in conjunction with Article 560^{7} § 2 sentence 3 CCP). In turn, in the absence of the possibility of putting the order granting the right to use things into effect in that manner, the order can be implemented by enforcement of non-pecuniary performance on the surrender of movable property (Article 560^{3a} § 9 CCP in conjunction with Article 560^{7} § 2 sentence 3 CCP).

The court's findings of fact forming the basis of a decision and the court's final order on the use of items do not bind the court in proceedings, the subject-matter of which is a request for surrender of items based on the ownership right (Article 560^{7} § 2 sentence 4 CCP). The court ruling on granting the right to use items can also apply to an applicant. Such a ruling makes it possible to use items without the need to take into account the right of ownership of them. As the legislator points out in Article 560^{7} § 2 CCP, the entitlement is temporary and serves exclusively to use the items in a manner determined by the court.

The possibility of taking items or domestic animals from the dwelling or its immediate surroundings after the court has issued an order obliging a perpetrator of domestic violence to vacate the jointly occupied dwelling and its immediate surroundings or prohibiting the perpetrator from approaching the jointly occupied dwelling and its immediate surroundings is introduced by Article 11a item 6 ACDV. It can only take place if the person experiencing violence agrees to it, with this possibility being limited to two cases. The police presence is then necessary (Article 11a item 6 ACDV), a person intending to recover items or animals submits a relevant application to the police (11a item 7 ACDV). The action is carried out on a specific date as a result of an agreement with the person experiencing violence, who can participate in the action or authorize another person to do so. However, where the person objects to the recovery of items or animals, they shall be left in the jointly occupied dwelling or in its immediate surroundings (Article 11a item 8 ACDV). In the event of an objection raised by the person experiencing violence, the request for the surrender of items can be asserted under the terms of the Civil Code, based on the right to the items of the perpetrator of violence.

5.4. Modification of an order

Under Article 523 CCP, a final and binding order as to substance cannot be modified or repealed, unless a specific provision provides otherwise. A final and binding order dismissing an application may be modified by the court if the circumstances of the case change.

Article 11ab ACDV provides for such a possibility in the case of an order obliging the perpetrator of violence to vacate the jointly occupied dwelling and its immediate surroundings or prohibiting the perpetrator from approaching the dwelling and its immediate surroundings or the person experiencing domestic violence, or prohibiting the perpetrator from contacting that person, or prohibiting the perpetrator from entering the premises of a school, educational, care, artistic, sports facility (attended by the person experiencing violence) or a workplace or any other locality in which that person habitually or regularly stays, accompanied by a prohibition on the perpetrator's presence on those premises.

The provisions of Article 11ab points 1-3 ACDV prescribe that, when examining a case on modifying or repealing such an order, the court take into account the circumstances of the victims of domestic violence and the perpetrators of that violence, including, in particular, information on the course and effects of the actions taken and documented in the procedure of "The Blue Card", provided that the procedure was carried out. It will be evidenced by the participation and the effects of participation in a correctional-educational and psychological-therapeutic programme for perpetrators of violence and the participation and the effects of participation in other forms of influencing, particularly in a therapy aimed at treating addiction. The court shall therefore examine the perpetrator's attitude and the correction of his/her conduct, including the course and effects of the blue card procedure, and the participation in an adequate correctional-educational or psychological-therapeutic programme for domestic violence perpetrators or in a treatment programme for substance abuse.[99]

It is argued that in the proceedings on repealing or modifying an order the court should take into account all the changed circumstances of the case and assess their impact on the issued decision. It is indicated that such proceedings can be carried out at the request of both a party – person experiencing violence or its perpetrator – and *ex officio*.[100] It is hard to accept in view of the content of Article 506 CCP, which requires

[99] S. Spurek, *Przeciwdziałanie przemocy domowej, Komentarz*, Warszawa 2023, marginal note 15 to Articles 11a,11aa,11ab, 15.

[100] A. Laskowska – Hulisz, *Postępowanie nieprocesowe*..., comment 13.

the legislator to include an explicit rule in a special provision regarding the permissibility of the court taking such action *ex officio* in the absence of a corresponding provision in the Code of Civil Procedure or the Act on Counteracting Domestic Violence.

It is also possible to reapply for obliging the perpetrator of violence to vacate the dwelling and its immediate surroundings or prohibit that perpetrator from approaching, contacting, entry – despite the final and binding nature of an order dismissing such a request – when the circumstances of the case have changed. A change of the ruling will involve the occurrence of acts of domestic violence. Article 523 sentence 2 CCP is the procedural basis for conducting new proceedings on claims regarding counteracting domestic violence.

A court-issued order obliging the perpetrator of violence to vacate the dwelling and its immediate surroundings or prohibiting the perpetrator from approaching, contacting, entry is significant for the protection from violence. It does not specify the period for which the perpetrator of violence is obliged to vacate the dwelling or the prohibitions are introduced. It follows from Article 560^7 § 2 CCP that the obligation is imposed indefinitely, with the possibility for the parties to demand that the order in this regard be modified or repealed if circumstances change. Authors have expressed criticism of the fact that no grounds for lifting such an obligation, no minimum time limit for its enforcement and no specific regulations for the procedure in this regard are indicated. Thus it may turn out that the obligation will be imposed on a perpetrator for life, which makes it more burdensome than a penal measure imposed on an offender.[101] Besides, a perpetrator of violence continues to have the right to the dwelling, thus the steps connected with regaining the possibility of using it can be taken.[102]

---

[101] M. Budyn-Kulik [in:] *Wzajemna relacja przepisów dotyczących nakazu opuszczenia przez sprawcę przemocy lokalu zajmowanego wspólnie z pokrzywdzonym (art. 41 k.k. i przepisy wprowadzone w tzw. tarczy antycovidowej), Prawo a stan epidemii*, eds. A. Górski, E. Sarnacka Białystok 2022, pp. 140-148; M. Budyn-Kulik [in:] *Kodeks wykroczeń Komentarz*, ed. Paweł Daniluk, Warszawa 2023, marginal note 6 to Article 66b.

[102] See the remarks contained in point 5.1.

Chapter VI

Enforcement proceedings

6.1. The nature of court enforcement

Enforcement cases are carried out by district courts and court enforcement officers attached to them (Article 758 CCP). Enforcement actions themselves are performed by court enforcement officers, with the exception of those reserved to the courts (Article 759 § 1 CCP). An enforceable title forms the basis for enforcement carried out based on the regulation of Part 3 of the Code of Civil Procedure. An enforcement title with an appended enforceability clause shall be an enforceable title, unless otherwise provided by law (Article 776 CCP).

In the case of rulings issued by the court with regard to a request based on the circumstances of the hypothesis of a legal norm laid down in the Act on Counteracting Domestic Violence, the Act refers to the method in which enforcement is carried out only in one case. Where an order obliging the perpetrator of violence to vacate the jointly occupied dwelling and its immediate surroundings or prohibiting the perpetrator from approaching the jointly occupied dwelling and its immediate surroundings is issued, Article 11a item 5 ACDV prescribes that the provisions on the enforcement of the obligation to clear the dwelling used to meet a debtor's housing needs shall apply accordingly to the performance of such an obligation. By contrast, there are no regulations regarding the enforcement (coercive implementation) of an order imposing a prohibition on approaching, contacting or entry.

To recall, enforcement aims to subordinate a debtor to the norm of substantive law within the limits determined in the enforceable title.[103] Such subordination allows for the use of force when it involves taking back a movable item or undertaking another action in an authoritative manner by enforcement authorities.[104] Enforcement authorities undertake those actions because they are entitled to the empire of State power,[105] which takes the form of enforcement in the procedural action.[106] This

---

[103] K. Korzan, *Zawieszenie a umorzenie postępowania egzekucyjnego,* Problemy Egzekucji Sądowej, 1994, No. VII, p. 5.
[104] K. Korzan, *Zawieszenie...,* p. 5.
[105] W. Tomalak, *Status ustrojowy i procesowy komornika sądowego*, Warsaw 2014, p. 129
[106] K. Korzan, *Zawieszenie...,* p. 5

coercion is manifested in a direct form, as in the case of the sale of items seized by a court enforcement officer, or in an indirect form by influencing the will of a debtor with coercive measures in the form of a fine in order to induce him/her to take the action specified in the content of an enforceable title [40]. Then an enforcement authority gains competence to put an enforceable title into effect in line with the content of a ruling contained in the enforcement title.

6.2. Enforcement of the obligation to vacate the dwelling

The legislator chose to place the regulation relating to the performance of actions permitting the compulsory enforcement of an obligation laid down in a court decision in the Act on Counteracting Domestic Violence. The provisions on the enforcement of the obligation to clear the dwelling used to meet a debtor's housing needs shall apply accordingly to a court-issued order obliging the perpetrator of violence to clear the jointly occupied dwelling and its immediate surroundings or prohibiting the perpetrator from approaching the dwelling and its immediate surroundings. These provisions are in Article 1046 CCP. Under Article 1046 § 1 CCP, if a debtor is to vacate a room, the court enforcement officer will call upon him/her to fulfil this obligation voluntarily within a time limit set adequately to the circumstances, and after its ineffective expiry, the court enforcement officer will take the actions necessary to give the creditor possession of the premises. However, in the case of dwelling, Article 1046 § 4 CCP contains further provisions that envisage the removal of the debtor to another dwelling or room to which he/she has a legal title and in which he/she can live, when the enforceable title does not give the debtor the right to conclude a social housing lease agreement or the right to alternative premises. Where a debtor does not have a legal title to another dwelling or room in which he/she can live, the court enforcement officer applies to the commune competent for the location of dwelling to be cleared to indicate temporary accommodation for the debtor. However, if the debtor is not even entitled to temporary accommodation, the court enforcement officer removes the debtor to a shelter, hostel or other facility providing overnight accommodation indicated by the commune – at the court enforcement officer's request (Article 1046 § 5^1 CCP). A perpetrator of domestic violence is not entitled to temporary accommodation. The Act on the Protection of Tenants' Rights, which introduces provisions related to granting a temporary room to a person obliged to clear the dwelling, excludes such an entitlement in respect of a perpetrator of domestic violence (Article 25d point 1 APTR).

Otherwise, a temporary accommodation lease agreement shall be concluded with a person in respect of whom enforcement has been initiated based on an enforceable title in which an obligation to clear the dwelling serving housing needs has been adjudicated, but without the right to conclude a social housing lease agreement or the right to alternative premises (Article 25c APTR). Similarly, it is inadmissible for the court to determine the entitlement of a perpetrator of violence to conclude a social housing lease agreement (Article 17 item 1 APTR). Moreover, in a situation of issuing an order obliging a perpetrator of violence to vacate the jointly occupied dwelling and its immediate surroundings, the protection afforded by Article 16 APTR, which prohibits the enforcement of such a decision during the winter period, i.e. from 1 November to 31 March of the following year, when an evicted person has not been indicated the premises to which he/she is to be rehoused (Article 17 item 1 APTR), has been excluded.

The Regulation of the Minister of Justice of 3 August 2023 on specific procedures for the enforcement of cases on the enforcement of an order obliging a perpetrator of violence to vacate the jointly occupied dwelling and its immediate surroundings[107] sets the time-limits for the court enforcement officer and the commune to take action and for the debtor to vacate the dwelling. But when all those time-limits are met, at least 18 days will elapse between the receipt of the enforcement request and the vacating of dwelling. Even the enforcement of a ruling on securing a claim by obliging the perpetrator to vacate the dwelling is not governed by any specific provisions allowing for the immediate removal of a perpetrator of domestic violence.

An element of the legal regulation intended to strengthen the protection of individuals affected by domestic violence is the service on such a person, as a creditor, of an enforcement title containing an order to vacate the jointly occupied dwelling and its immediate surroundings with an enforceability clause appended *ex officio* by the court (Article 782 § 1^1 CCP). It is another facilitation for the effective and swift isolation of the perpetrator of violence. Notably, the Code of Civil Procedure does not envisage appending an enforceability clause to a prohibition on approaching the dwelling, even though both decisions are contained in the operative part of the court order.

Attention should be paid to the content of Article 560^7 § 1 CCP, where the wording of the obligation to vacate the dwelling was introduced, whereas Article 1046 CCP contains the expression "clearing the dwelling", which Article 11a item 5 refers to. The different wording in the operative part of a court order, therefore, refers to the

[107] Journal of Laws 2023, item 1568.

performance of an obligation, which amounts to the conduct of leaving the dwelling. It follows from the further part of Article 1046 CCP that if a debtor is to clear the dwelling serving his/her residential needs, the court enforcement officer shall summon him/her to fulfil this obligation voluntarily within a time limit to be set according to the circumstances. If the time limit expires without results, the court enforcement officer shall take such steps as are necessary to put the creditor in possession of dwelling (Article 1046 § 1 CCP). However, if the court order is implemented, it will not be necessary for the creditor, a family member affected by violence, to enter the dwelling. Even a situation where such a person vacated the dwelling due to the perpetrator's conduct (Article 11a item 2 point 1 ACDV) will be connected with that person's return to the dwelling, not its recovery.

6.3. Enforcement of a prohibition regarding conduct

Article 782 CCP does not have any provision on appending an enforceability clause *ex officio* to an enforcement title and serving it on the creditor, which imposes on a perpetrator of violence a prohibition on approaching the dwelling and its immediate surroundings or other prohibitions such as: a prohibition on approaching, contacting or entry.

Consequently, in the event of any other ruling on protection from violence – apart from the obligation to vacate the dwelling and its surroundings – a person affected by violence will be obliged to perform further acts of legal procedure. It becomes necessary to obtain an enforceable title and only then to initiate enforcement proceedings. As indicated above, in that case the legislator does not provide for a method of enforcement nor lay down any provisions that would enable enforcement actions to be carried out swiftly and efficiently. A court-issued decision with a designated standard of conduct of a participant in the proceedings in the form of a prohibition on approaching the dwelling and its immediate surroundings; a prohibition on approaching the person experiencing violence; a prohibition on contacting the person experiencing violence; a prohibition on entering the premises of a school, educational, care, artistic, sports facility attended by the person experiencing domestic violence or a workplace or any other locality in which that person habitually or regularly stays, accompanied by a prohibition on the perpetrator's presence on those premises – will therefore require a search for a way to enforce the court's decision compulsorily.

Generally, the right to the court in the constitutional sense consists of the right of access to a court, the right to an adequate judicial procedure and the right to a court judgment. The right to the court must be seen not only in terms of the possibility of delivering a court ruling but also the possibility of enforcing it. The task of the legislator is to create a normative situation in which the right to a judgment following a fair hearing and the possibility of its enforcement are ensured [42].

Given that the range of coercive measures serving to enforce the obligation of conduct laid down in a court ruling is a closed set, the Code of Civil Procedure must be examined for the purpose of accepting an argument for the admissibility of an adequate coercive measure from among that set of measures, in view of the content of a court decision obliging the perpetrator of violence to behave appropriately. In doing so, the enforcement authority is not entitled to examine the legitimacy and enforceability of the obligation covered by the enforceable title (Article 804 § 1 CCP).

Inasmuch as Article 11a item 5 ACDV refers to the application, *mutatis mutandis*, of the provisions on the enforcement of an obligation to clear the dwelling serving a debtor's housing needs to an order obliging a perpetrator of violence to vacate the jointly occupied dwelling and its immediate vicinity or prohibiting the perpetrator from approaching the dwelling and its immediate vicinity, there is no regulation in the area of coercive enforcement of a prohibition on approaching, contacting or entering certain localities. Despite the content of Article 11a item 5 ACDV, it will be possible to carry out enforcement actions involving the clearing of dwelling to enforce the court's ruling prohibiting the perpetrator from approaching it.

It must be emphasised that the enforcement in such a case must be carried out while ensuring the protection of the debtor's rights, which should take place already at the level of the generally expressed right to the court. The guarantee of the right to the court, by ensuring the proper course of proceedings at the stage of enforcement of a court decision, is intended to ensure the protection of the rights of any actor being a debtor [13]. It will take place regardless of whether the court will carry out enforcement itself or will only supervise its course.

The applied coercive measures cannot involve greater hardship for the debtor than is strictly necessary to ensure that the conduct introduced in the enforceable title is implemented. The applied coercive measures must be the ones that are prescribed by the provisions of Part Three of the Code of Civil Procedure. And the sheer intensity of the applied measure must not in any case go beyond the achievement of the purpose of the undertaken action, which is putting the enforcement title into effect.

The standard set out in the wording of a court order is a performance in the form of refraining from certain actions. The enforcement of such an order will be carried out pursuant to Article 1051§ 1 CCP. It prescribes that in the event that a debtor has acted in breach of his/her obligation, although he/she was obliged to refrain from a certain action, the court shall impose a fine on him/her. Enforcement proceedings shall in this case be conducted by the court in whose district the debtor acted contrary to his/her obligation (Article 1051 § 1 sentence 1 CCP). Under Article 1052 sentences 1 and 2 CCP, in a single order, the court may impose a fine not exceeding 15,000 zlotys, unless the imposition of a fine has already proved ineffective twice. On the other hand, the total sum of fines may not exceed one million zlotys. A further enforcement measure is the conversion of a fine into a detention, counting one day of detention as 50 to 1,500 zlotys of the fine, in the event of the debtor's failure to pay, although the total duration of the detention may not exceed six months. This conversion shall be decided by the court in an order imposing a fine (Article 1053 §1 CCP).

At the same time, Article 1051^1 § 1 CCP provides for – instead of imposing a fine – ordering the debtor to pay the creditor a defined sum of money for having committed a breach of specific conduct, together with a threat of ordering the payment of a specific sum of money for each subsequent breach of the obligation. In determining the amount of money, the court should take into account the interests of the parties to such an extent as to ensure that the obligation set out in the enforceable title is enforceable and that the debtor is not burdened beyond what is necessary (Article 1050^1 § 4 in conjunction with Article 1051^1 § 3 CCP).

The court order on a payment to the creditor – a person experiencing violence – is an enforceable title in favour of that creditor without appending an enforceability clause. This makes it possible to apply to a court enforcement officer to enforce the pecuniary provision from all of the debtor's assets (Article 803 CCP). The enforcement will be carried out using all the methods provided for in the Code of Civil Procedure in the case of pecuniary enforcement together with enforcement against the debtor's immovable property, upon request by the creditor (Article 799 § 1 CCP).

The protection of a creditor is significantly increased in that case because of the permissibility of charging the debtor with another sum to be paid to the creditor. The court, when ordering the payment to the creditor of a specified sum of money for a committed breach, shall at the same time rule on the threat of payment of a specified sum of money for each subsequent breach of the obligation (Article 1051^1 § 1 CCP). At the request of the creditor, the court may increase the sum of money due to the creditor from the debtor (Article 1050^{1} § 2 sentence 4 CCP in conjunction with Article 1051^{1} § 3 CCP).

Once it is established that the debtor has continued to act in breach of his/her obligation, the court shall, at the request of the creditor, order the debtor to pay to the creditor the sum of money arising from the contents of the earlier order in which this possibility was reserved. The order can be re-issued (Article 1051^{1} § 2 CCP) and, similarly to a first court decision imposing an obligation to pay a sum of money, will be enforceable without the need for an enforceability clause (Article 1050^{1} § 2 sentence 3 CCP in conjunction with Article 1051^{1} § 3 CCP). Moreover, at the request of the creditor, the court may oblige the debtor to provide security for damage threatening the creditor by virtue of the debtor's continued breach of his/her obligation, together with an indication of the amount and duration of the security (Article 1051 § 2 CCP).

It seems that the enforcement of the obligation to vacate the dwelling in accordance with the provisions of Article 1046 CCP – on the obligation to clear the room – taking into account the content of the Regulation of the Minister of Justice, makes it possible to ensure the protection of a person experiencing violence. Similarly, Articles 1051 CCP and 1051^{1} CCP accompanied by a rather substantial financial burden on the debtor (the perpetrator of violence) during the performance of the obligation not to engage in domestic violence are an adequate safeguard for such protection. Doubts are raised only by the content of Article 782 § 1^{1} CCP. This is because the court grants an *ex officio* enforceability clause to an enforcement title requiring a perpetrator of violence to vacate the jointly occupied dwelling and its immediate surroundings (which allows for the initiation of enforcement). However, the court is no longer obliged to do so in respect of a prohibition on approaching the dwelling and other prohibitions connected with protection from violence issued in a ruling. A second enforceable title will have to be obtained. The first title is served *ex officio* by the court (Article 782 § 1^{1} sentence 2 CCP) for an enforcement to be carried by a court enforcement officer based on an order to vacate the premises, and the second, which must be requested by the creditor, for an enforcement to be carried out by the court based on an order regarding conduct that requires the debtor – the perpetrator of violence – to refrain from certain conduct.

Regardless of the regulations envisaged in enforcement proceedings, action undertaken by the public prosecutor to initiate such proceedings or steps taken to enforce effectively the conduct of a perpetrator of violence would be of importance. The legislator did not envisage any action by the prosecutor in enforcement proceedings as regards the coercive enforcement of the obligation and prohibition(s) laid down in a court order. In fact, it is another stage of the protection of household members from acts of violence. The efficiently performed enforcement action will help to protect household members from acts of violence. It is particularly important in the case of an issued prohibition on approaching the dwelling and its immediate surroundings, prohibition on approaching the person experiencing violence, prohibition on contacting that person, prohibition on entering the premises of a school, educational, care, artistic, sports facility attended by the person experiencing domestic violence or a workplace or any other locality in which that person habitually or regularly stays, accompanied by a prohibition on the perpetrator's presence on those premises.

The above issues of carrying out the enforcement of a court-issued obligation to vacate the dwelling or a prohibition on approaching it accompanied by the issuing of prohibitions on approach, contact or entry, and the enforcement of an order on securing such a claim, or even an act issued by a police officer containing an order to vacate the dwelling and a prohibition on approaching it with further prohibitions on approach, contact and entry, should be juxtaposed with the issue of strengthening the protection of household members provided by a new petty offence introduced into the Petty Offences Code in Article 66b POC.[108] Of particular importance at this point is the decision by the legislator to include this offence in the proceedings under the expedited procedure, as prescribed by Article 90 § 2a Petty Offences Procedure Code. It allows the police to detain a person non-complying with an issued obligation or prohibition and caught in the act of committing a petty offence or immediately afterwards (Article 45 § 1 point 1 Petty Offences Procedure Code).

The duration of a person's detention shall be counted from the moment they are apprehended and shall not exceed 48 hours (Article 46 § 6 Petty Offences Procedure Code). It will indeed be an act of separating a perpetrator of violence, who still poses a threat in terms of action bearing the hallmarks of violence, from the household members.

These actions will be supplemented by the permissibility of detaining a perpetrator of violence posing an imminent threat to human life or health (Article 15a item 1 PA) with the existing general area of police power of detention (Article 15 item 1 point 2 PA). Under this entitlement, the police can only detain a person who clearly poses an imminent threat to human life or health (Article 15 item 1 point 3 PA). In the absence of any further grounds for such detention, it will be admissible irrespective of the pending court proceedings on a request for obliging a perpetrator of violence to vacate the dwelling and prohibiting the perpetrator from approaching it, an issued order on

---

[1] Article 1051

securing such a claim or an enforceable ruling containing such an obligation, and also in the duration of a police order and prohibition(s).

Chapter VII

Summary

7.1. Statistical data

Before a summary of the analysis of domestic violence and drawing conclusions from it, it will be important to provide basic data on domestic violence.[109] The statistical data published by the police show that in 2022 there was a decline in the number of cases of family violence. In 2022, 131,813 incidents involving particular types of violence were reported. Compared to 2021, it was a decline by 9,596 cases, whereas compared to 2020, it was a decline by 32,252 cases.

As regards the type of violence, the incidents reported in 2022 can be broken down into: 47,405 cases of physical violence, 64,624 – mental, 1,758 – sexual, 1,630 – economic and 16 396 cases of violence of other type.

The statistical data for 2022 show that the most frequent type of domestic violence is mental violence, which accounted for 49.03% of the overall number of cases of domestic violence, whereas physical violence ranked second – 35,96%.

The statistical data for 2022 show that women were the largest group of people suspected of being victims of domestic violence – 51,935 individuals, which accounted for 72.50% of the total number of individuals affected by such violence. 10,982 minors were affected by such violence. Finally, 8,714 men were affected by violence.

In 2022, in total 2,101 applications were submitted to the court for obliging the perpetrator of violence to vacate the jointly occupied dwelling and its immediate surroundings or prohibiting the perpetrator from approaching the dwelling and its immediate surroundings. 1,052 rulings were delivered on obliging the perpetrator of violence to vacate the jointly occupied dwelling and its immediate surroundings or to

[109]https://www.gov.pl/web/rodzina/sprawozdanie-z-realizacji-krajowego-programu-przeciwdzialania-przemocy-w-rodzinie-za-rok-2022. A report for 2023 has not been published by the time this study goes to print. It will be available at the address: https://www.gov.pl/web/rodzina/sprawozdanie-z-realizacji-krajowego-programu-przeciwdzialania-przemocy-w-rodzinie-za-rok-2024.

prohibit the perpetrator from approaching the dwelling and its immediate surroundings. Moreover, courts delivered 456 judgements on eviction due to the use of family violence.

7.2. Conclusions

The wide range of legal regulations currently relating to situations that involve incidents of domestic violence – expressed in a legal definition of this concept – is intended to ensure household members protection from acts of violence. The introduction of actions aimed at isolating the perpetrator of violence from the household members was fundamental to the creation of that guarantee. These actions are to be carried out swiftly, without the introduction of numerous procedural acts designed to demonstrate a very high degree of probability that incidents involving violence have occurred. If the protection of individuals affected by violence is to ensure safety, the decision on the isolation of the perpetrator should be taken at the scene, after the circumstances have been clarified and assumed to exist with a high degree of probability, which is possible because of a limited number of evidentiary measures and the reduced degree of formalism in the conduct of evidence proceedings.

Clearly, it is indispensable for individuals affected by violence, which is also a threat to their life or health, to eliminate the possibility of the perpetrator repeating the violent action. The protection of household members is guaranteed not only by the removal of the perpetrator from the dwelling, but also by a prohibition on approaching the dwelling or the individuals affected by violence, a non-harassment order, or a prohibition on entering the places where they study, work out, develop their interests. It gives a sense of existing psychological safety. Generally, the mere fear of the possibility of a repetition of violent actions is a significant psychological burden, which is an element of violence itself. Life in fear about every moment that may bring further acts of violence can result in significant mental harm to those who have experienced violent acts.

Therefore, it was so important to introduce into the Police Act the authority of any police officer to issue a legal instrument ordering a person using violence to vacate immediately the jointly occupied dwelling and immediate surroundings and prohibiting that person from approaching the jointly occupied dwelling and its immediate surroundings.

A police intervention in a dwelling where such incidents occur allows for taking immediate actions not only to apprehend the violent person, which must be connected with an imminent threat to the life or health of the household members, but also in the case of a mere threat to the life or health of the person affected by violence. It is crucial to reintroduce the previous entitlement of the police to issue an order to vacate the dwelling or a prohibition on approaching the dwelling instead of the provision introduced into the Police Act on issuing an order to vacate the dwelling and a prohibition on approaching it, which involves a different assessment of the facts as a basis for issuing the relevant content of an administrative act. The mere difficulty in establishing and assessing facts by a police officer cannot lead to an additional burden on the perpetrator of violence.

The significantly reduced course of examination proceedings with the issuing of an order and prohibition regarding conduct subject to immediate compulsory enforcement, with the possibility of initiating enforcement actions carried out in a simplified manner, together with the admissibility of direct coercion, lays the foundations for guaranteeing swift and efficient protection for a person affected by violence. At the same time, a perpetrator of violence has been guaranteed access to the court to examine the legality, correctness and legitimacy of an issued decision. On the other hand, the continued validity – after the expiry of 14 days – of an order to vacate immediately the jointly occupied dwelling and its immediate surroundings and a prohibition on approaching the jointly occupied dwelling and its immediate surroundings is possible only based on a ruling of an ordinary court. It is true that most objections have been raised to this section of the legislation, but even without amending the current rules, it would be possible to remove these legislative shortcomings.

We should call for the increased activity of the public prosecutor at the stage of court protection proceedings. The prosecutor's authority in the Code of Civil Procedure to initiate or participate in any proceedings also gives the prosecutor the power to initiate protection proceedings so that the court issues an order extending the validity of a police-issued order and prohibition. The prosecutor's activity in the area of protection proceedings and examination proceedings carried out by the court would truly further enhance the area of safety created to protect household members from domestic violence. The prosecutor's help would be significant even during the submission of an application for securing a claim, initiation of examination proceedings, at the stage of the enforcement of an enforceable title. Therefore, the prosecutor, whose action in judicial or enforcement proceedings should be based on taking action to protect the rule of law, citizens' rights or the public interest (as prescribed by Article 7 CCP), would strive to eliminate action of people who would try to make use of legal regulations on counteracting domestic violence for other purposes. Making such a request would be an abuse of procedural law (Article 4^1 CCP), and it should lead to a refusal to carry out proceedings and grant legal protection to a party. This area of the prosecutor's action is also significant for a person in respect of whom action was taken with an attempt to use the institute of legal protection from violence. The prosecutor would be an entity, driven only by the grounds indicated in Article 7 CCP, who lodges a complaint against a police-issued order and prohibition, or a complaint against an order on security, or lodges an appeal against a court ruling obliging the alleged perpetrator of violence to vacate the dwelling or to refrain from undertaking action based on the prohibitions provided for in the Act on Counteracting Domestic Violence.

The further shortcomings in providing protection have been indicated in the analysis of the measures for counteracting violence. Nevertheless, the legislator's efforts to create legal protection for individuals affected by domestic violence should be evaluated positively, bearing in mind that they are at the same time the implementation of the Istanbul Convention.

Bibliography

1. Adamiak B., *Zagadnienia ogólne procesowego prawa administracyjnego* [in:] *System prawa administracyjnego, Vol. 9. Prawo procesowe administracyjne*, eds. R. Hauser, Z. Niewiadomski, A. Wróbel Warsaw 2020
2. Adamiak B., *Postępowanie administracyjne i sądowoadministracyjn*e, Warsaw 2021
3. Bieńkowska E., Mazowiecka L., *Konwencja o zapobieganiu i zwalczaniu przemocy domowej wobec kobiet,* Warsaw 2016
4. Bielecki L. [in:] *Prawo administracyjne Część ogólna, ustrojowe prawo administracyjne, wybrane zagadnienia materialnego prawa administracyjnego*, eds. M. Zdyb, J. Stelmasiak, Warsaw 2016
5. Budyn-Kulik M. [in:] *Wzajemna relacja przepisów dotyczących nakazu opuszczenia przez sprawcę przemocy lokalu zajmowanego wspólnie z pokrzywdzonym (art. 41 k.k. i przepisy wprowadzone w tzw. tarczy antycovidowej), Prawo a stan epidemii*, eds. A. Górski, E. Sarnacka Białystok 2022
6. Budyn-Kulik M. [in:] *Kodeks wykroczeń Komentarz*, ed. Paweł Daniluk, Warszawa 2023
7. Burtowy M., *Nowa procedura szybkiego reagowania wobec sprawców przemocy domowej*, Lex/el 2020
8. Gizbert – Studnicki T., *Wykładnia celowościowa*, Studia Prawnicze 1985, manuscript 3-4
9. Grzegorczyk P., Weitz K. [in:] *Konstytucja RP. T. 1. Komentarz. Art. 1–86*. eds. M. Safjan, L. Bosek, Warsaw 2016
10. Flaga – Gieruszyńska K. [in:] *Kodeks postępowania cywilnego Postępowanie zabezpieczające*, ed. J. Gołaczyński, Warsaw 2021
11. Hauser A., Piątek W., Paduch A., Skoczylas A. [in:] *Postępowanie administracyjne i sądowoadministracyjne*, eds. A. Hauser, A. Skoczylas, Warsaw 2021
12. Hauser R., Leoński Z., *Postępowanie egzekucyjne w administracji. Komentarz*, eds. R. Hauser, A. Skoczylas, Warsaw 2014
13. Jagieła J., *Nakazanie przez Policję osobie stosującej przemoc w rodzinie opuszczenie wspólnie zajmowanego mieszkania i jego bezpośredniego otoczenia lub zakazanie zbliżania się do mieszkania i jego bezpośredniego*

otoczenia [in:] *Symbolae Andreae Marciniak dedicatae*, eds. J Jagieła, R. Kulski, Warsaw 2022

14. Janik M [in:] *Administracja Prawo administracyjne Część ogólna*, eds. J. Blicharz, L. Zacharko, Katowice 2018
15. Jodłowski J., *Kilka kwestii z teorii międzynarodowego postępowania cywilnego*, PiP 1974, No. 2
16. Karaźniewicz J. [in:] *Ustawa o Policji. Komentarz*, eds. K. Chałubińska-Jentkiewicz, J. Kurek, Warsaw 2021
17. Kiełtyka A., Ważny A., *Przeciwdziałanie przemocy w rodzinie. Komentarz*, A. Kiełtyka, A. Ważny, Warsaw 2015
18. Kledzik P. [in:] Postępowanie administracyjne, egzekucyjne i sądowoadministracyjne, ed. M. Wierzbowski, Warsaw 2022
19. Kmiecik Z., *Wszczęcie ogólnego postępowania administracyjnego*, Warsaw 2014
20. Kotowski W., *Ustawa o Policji. Komentarz* , Lex Online 2024
21. Korzan K., *Zawieszenie a umorzenie postępowania egzekucyjnego,* Problemy Egzekucji Sądowej, 1994, No. VII,
22. Laskowska – Hulisz A., *Postępowanie nieprocesowe w sprawach o zobowiązanie osoby stosującej przemoc w rodzinie do opuszczenia wspólnie zajmowanego mieszkania i jego bezpośredniego otoczenia lub zakazanie zbliżania się do mieszkania i jego bezpośredniego otoczenia*, *Komentarz*, Lex/el 2020
23. Lubiński K., *Pojęcie i zakres wymiaru sprawiedliwości*, Studia Prawnicze 1987, No. 4
24. Łabuz P. [in:] *Ustawa o Policji Komentarz*, ed. A. Choromańska, Warsaw 2022
25. Manikowski F., *Postępowanie w sprawie o zobowiązania osoby stosującej przemoc w rodzinie do opuszczenia wspólnie zajmowanego mieszkania i jego bezpośredniego otoczenia lub zakazania zbliżania się do mieszkania i jego bezpośredniego otoczenia - analiza badań aktowych*, Prawo w działaniu. Sprawy cywilne, 2022, No. 50
26. Markiewicz K., *Zasady orzekania w postępowaniu nieprocesowym*, Warszawa 2013
27. Nowacki J., *„Odpowiednie" stosowanie; Analogia legis*, Warsaw 1966
28. Ochendowski E., *Prawo administracyjne część ogólna*, Toruń 2013
29. Olszanowski J. [in:] *Postępowanie administracyjne i sądowoadministracyjne*, eds. A. Hauser, A. Skoczylas, Warsaw 2021
30. Pierzchała E [in:] *Administracja Prawo administracyjne Część ogólna*, eds. J. Blicharz, L. Zacharko, Katowice 2018

31. Piskozub P., *Izolacja sprawcy przemocy w rodzinie*, Legalis/el 2021
32. Przybysz P., *Postępowanie egzekucyjne w administracji. Komentarz.* Warsaw 2021
33. Radwanowicz-Wanczewska J. [in:] *Ustawa o postępowaniu egzekucyjnym w administracji. Komentarz*, ed. D. Kijowski, Lex/el 2015
34. Sawczyn W., *Postępowanie egzekucyjne w administracji. Komentarz*. eds. R. Hauser, M. Wierzbowski, Warsaw 2024
35. Spurek S., *Przeciwdziałanie przemocy w rodzinie Komentarz,* Warsaw 2019
36. Spurek S., *Nasza Konwencja*, Brussels 2023
37. Spurek S., *Przeciwdziałanie przemocy domowej, Komentarz*, Warszawa 2023
38. Szewczyk E., Szewczyk M., *Generalny akt administracyjny między indywidualnym aktem administracyjnym a aktem normatywnym*. Warsaw 2014
39. Tarno J.P. [in:] W. Chruścielewski, J.P. Tarno, P. Dańczak, *Postępowanie administracyjne i postępowanie przed sądami administracyjnymi*, Warsaw 2018
40. Tomalak W., *Status ustrojowy i procesowy komornika sądowego*, Warsaw 2014
41. Wiktorska P., *Procedury prawne związane z możliwościami odseparowania sprawcy przemocy domowej od osoby doświadczającej przemocy*, Prawo w działaniu Sprawy karne 2021, No. 45
42. Wolwiak I., *Odpowiednie stosowanie przepisów o procesie do samodzielnego postępowania uregulowanego w KPC*, Monitor Prawniczy 2021, No. 8
43. Wolwiak I., *Zabezpieczenie rodziny przed przemocą w następstwie wydanego przez Policję nakazu opuszczenia mieszkania bądź zbliżania się do niego*, Acta Univeristatis Lodziensis Folia Iuridica , special numer, 2023
44. Woś P., *Postępowanie wobec osoby stosującej przemoc w rodzinie w Kodeksie postępowania cywilnego*, Studia Prawnicze KUL 2023, No. 1
45. Wrona G., *Ustawa o przeciwdziałaniu przemocy w rodzinie. Komentarz*, Legalis/el 2021
46. Wrona G. [in:] *Przeciwdziałanie przemocy domowej – analiza zmian*, P. Piskozub, G. Wrona, Warsaw 2023
47. Wróblewski J. [in:] *Jerzy Wróblewski pisma wybrane*, wybór i wstęp M. Zirk-Sadowski, Warsaw 2015
48. Zdyb M., *Istota decyzji*, Lublin 1993

Contents

www.ingramcontent.com/pod-product-compliance
Lightning Source LLC
LaVergne TN
LVHW010459160826
845677LV00012B/2562